TOP 20 DAREDEVILS

DAREDEVILS

★ COUNTDOWN TO DANGER

FOR MAX, OUR FAVORITE DATA SCIENTIST.
-M.B. AND G.B.

Library of Congress Cataloging-in-Publication Data available

ISBN 978-1-338-25337-5

10 9 8 7 6 5 4 3 2 1   19 20 21 22 23

Printed in the U.S.A.   40
First printing 2019

Book design by Sunny Lee
Photo Research by Cian O'Day

TOP 20 DAREDEVILS

★ COUNTDOWN TO DANGER

BY MELVIN
& GILDA BERGER
ART BY
BERAT PEKMEZCI

TABLE of CONTENTS

20 MABEL STARK

THE TIGER IS THE ROYAL LORD OF ALL ANIMAL CREATION. . . . TO ME HE IS THE MOST MAGNIFICENT EXPRESSION OF ANIMAL LIFE.

BORN:
DECEMBER 9, 1889,
PRINCETON, KENTUCKY

CLAIM TO FAME:
TIGER TRAINER

DIED:
APRIL 20, 1968,
THOUSAND OAKS,
CALIFORNIA

BEFORE THE TIGERS...

Mabel Stark was born as Mary Haynie in Kentucky to poor tobacco farmers. She later changed her name to Mabel Stark. As a youngster, Mabel enjoyed watching the animals at the zoo. When she was 13, her parents passed away and friends shipped Mabel off to live with an aunt. But she wasn't happy there. At age 18, after taking a short course in nursing, she left home to work in a hospital. Sometime around 1911, Mabel met Al G. Barnes, who owned a circus in California. He offered her a job riding horses and training goats. But Stark wasn't satisfied with this work. Her heart was set on something more daring . . .

ACT 1   CRAZY ABOUT TIGERS

Mabel Stark just loved tigers. She had the greatest respect and admiration for them. So when she heard that the circus's tiger trainer had recently been killed, she begged for the job.

MABEL STARK AT RINGLING BROS. AND BARNUM & BAILEY CIRCUS, 1925

The circus's big-cat trainer, Louis Roth, taught Mabel how to parade the tigers and run them in circles. Mabel made them growl, swipe the air with their paws, roll over, and leap onto platforms around the cage. Instead of whipping them if they misbehaved, she rewarded good behavior with hunks of meat. After each trick, Mabel waved her hand. It was her way of thanking them for their performance. By 1916, Mabel Stark was the superstar of the show's tiger act.

JOKE

WHAT DID THE TIGER SAY AFTER EATING A COMEDIAN?

THAT TASTED FUNNY.

DID YOU KNOW?

Traveling circuses were once a major source of entertainment. And animal trainers were often the star performers! For thousands of years, people used animals for entertainment. Ancient rulers kept wild creatures as a sign of their power and wealth. Romans pitted men, known as gladiators, against animals in huge arenas before many spectators. Wealthy people exhibited tigers and other captured wild animals in exhibits called menageries. By 1831, wild-animal performances were popular acts in circuses and in sideshows. Some traveling shows built entire performances around animal trainers and their animals!

THE TIGER TUSSLE

Mabel trained her tiger cub, Rajah, to do her most famous stunt—the tiger wrestle. Here's how it worked:

1 She called Rajah inside the big cage where she did her act.

2 He ran over, rose on his hind legs, and put his front feet around her neck.

3 Then he pulled her to the ground and grabbed her head, all the while growling loudly as they wrestled on the ground.

STARK AND RAJAH, 1931

Audience members feared that she would be killed. Some shouted for help. Children cried. But Mabel broke free of the tiger's grip and jumped to her feet. There was stunned silence and then great applause. Mabel had wrestled with a tiger—and escaped with her life!

Tiger Tips

⭐ The tiger is the largest member of the cat family.

⭐ Wild tigers live only in Asia and Russia.

⭐ Tigers have long, orange-red coats with white bellies and mostly black-and-white-striped tails.

⭐ An average male tiger weighs about 420 pounds; an average female tiger weighs about 300 pounds.

⭐ There were once nine different kinds of tigers, but today there are only six—and they are all endangered.

⭐ In the early 1900s there were about 100,000 tigers in the wild. Today there are only about 3,000 to 4,500.

⭐ In a TV poll of 50,000 Animal Planet viewers from 73 countries, the tiger was voted the world's favorite animal, narrowly beating the dog.

DEFYING DEATH!

Can you imagine getting attacked by a tiger? How about TWO tigers?!
Well, that's exactly what happened to Mabel one rainy day in 1928.

The animals had spent the day on wet straw in their cages, and there had not
been time to feed them before the show began. Two of Mabel's tigers seemed
particularly upset. They filed into the giant cage, heads hanging low. They were
panting and barking. Mud had seeped into their paws, probably making them sore
and painful. Then the tiger named Zoo climbed onto the
wrong pedestal. He took the place of the tiger named Sheik,
who appeared to blame Mabel for the mix-up. Sheik leaped
forward and clawed Mabel's left thigh! The gash was so
deep it went through to the bone! Mabel continued as
though nothing had happened.

A helper opened and
rattled the cage door—a
signal for Sheik to leave
the cage. But the door
swung open too wide and
hit Zoo! Zoo jumped from
his pedestal and pulled
Mabel to the ground. As
she fell, Sheik struck out
with his paw. The blow
caught the side of her
head. Zoo growled and
bit Mabel's leg. Mabel
pulled out the gun she
kept in the cage for
emergencies. She fired
several blank cartridges
into Zoo's face, driving
him away. Terrified
workers nudged the
animals into their cages
and rushed Mabel to the
hospital.

Stark spent the next two years in and out of the hospital. Her broken body slowly mended, and her thoughts turned to getting back into the ring with her beloved tigers. Mabel never blamed the tigers when something went wrong; she only blamed herself. Perhaps they were hungry or in pain. Mabel always found a way to explain the tigers' bad behavior.

AN ANIMAL LOVER'S LEGACY

Mabel Stark became a symbol for women. Her life made people look at women in entertainment differently. She set an example for women who wished to work in occupations that were usually reserved for men. At a time when women were fighting to get the vote, Mabel Stark was known as a "new woman."

While daring animal acts thrilled audiences, they often harmed the animals in the process. Lions and tigers were trained to roar and hit their trainers, who then fought them off with whips and chairs. The animals were often beaten, starved, and had their teeth pulled to make them less dangerous. In the 1950s, people began objecting to this type of animal cruelty. And Mabel had a lot to do with the change in attitude and behavior. She helped people gain a higher regard for wild animals and their rights. She put an end to harsh animal training with whips and punishment. And she advanced the protection of endangered species.

JOKE

WHAT DO YOU CALL A TIGER TRAINER WHO PUTS HER RIGHT ARM IN A TIGER'S MOUTH?

LEFTY.

STARK TRAINING GOLDIE, CALIFORNIA, 1961

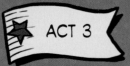 ACT 3

MABEL'S LAST ACT

When Mabel's animal show closed, she got a stunt job in Hollywood taking the place of actors in scenes where they were attacked by tigers. Then, in 1938, Stark took her last job. She performed as an animal trainer at a zoo and amusement park called Jungleland. In 1968, Jungleland was sold to new owners, who dropped her act. Mabel once said that without the snarling and roaring of striped cats leaping at her or each other, life wouldn't be worth living. At 79 years old, out of work and out of luck, the stouthearted Mabel Stark stayed true to her word and retired. Three months later, she died.

19 KITTY O'NEIL

> SCARED? WHAT FOR? I LOVE DANGER.

BORN:
MARCH 24, 1946,
CORPUS CHRISTI, TEXAS

CLAIM TO FAME:
TV & MOVIE STUNT PERFORMER

PRESENT HOME:
EUREKA,
SOUTH DAKOTA

BEFORE THE MOVIES...

Kitty O'Neil was born to a Cherokee mother and an Irish father. Shortly after her birth, her father died, so she was raised by her mother. At four months of age, Kitty fell ill with measles, mumps, and smallpox—all at the same time! Eventually, she recovered, but she was never the same. Kitty no longer reacted to sounds. Finally, when Kitty was two years old, a doctor found the cause of the change. The child could not hear! Kitty's loss of hearing was probably due to her early sicknesses. But Kitty's deafness didn't stop her from learning to speak. In fact, Kitty even learned to play the piano!

Despite being hearing impaired, Kitty showed her spunky spirit as early as age four. Kitty used to speed down her grandmother's long, dark, curvy laundry chute as if it were a playground slide! By age 12, Kitty was competing in swim races and often taking first prize. By 16, she went to California to study diving with a famous coach. This was just the beginning of Kitty's attempts to break records . . .

FASTEST WOMAN ON WATER

After diving, waterskiing became Kitty's great passion. Skimming along the surface of the water at high speeds requires both good balance and great strength. It also takes great courage. Kitty's love of speed and competition led her to want to break records. In 1970, she set a speed record for women's waterskiing at 104.85 miles per hour!

DID YOU KNOW?

In waterskiing, a person wearing special wide skis is pulled by a motorboat on the water surface. It was added as a demonstration sport in the 1972 Olympics.

FASTEST WOMAN ON LAND

Around the same time, Kitty began racing motorcycles and cars. In 1976, Kitty drove a special rocket-powered race car across a dry lake bed in Oregon. Her goal? To beat the world land speed record for women. The engine of her car produced 48,000 horsepower, hundreds of times the horsepower of an average car. On December 4, 1976, she set a new world record at 322 miles per hour.

Kitty tried nine more times to beat her own record. She finally succeeded in setting a new women's world land speed record of 512.70 miles per hour—nearly 200 miles per hour faster than the record she set two days earlier. Kitty O'Neil was the fastest woman in the world!

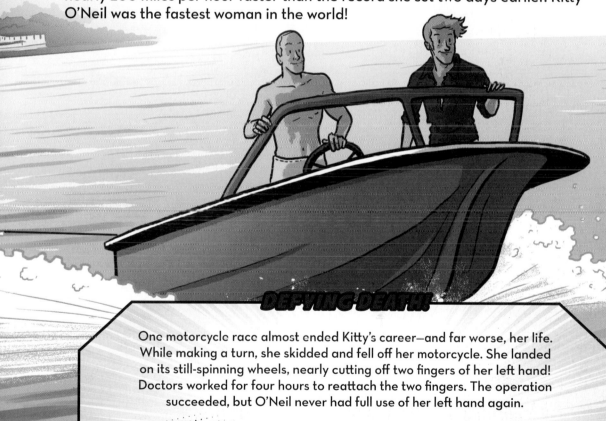

DEFYING DEATH!

One motorcycle race almost ended Kitty's career—and far worse, her life. While making a turn, she skidded and fell off her motorcycle. She landed on its still-spinning wheels, nearly cutting off two fingers of her left hand! Doctors worked for four hours to reattach the two fingers. The operation succeeded, but O'Neil never had full use of her left hand again.

JOKE

HOW MANY STUNTPEOPLE DO YOU NEED TO SCREW IN A LIGHTBULB?

TWO. ONE TO HOLD THE BULB, THE OTHER TO TURN THE LADDER.

THE HEIGHTS OF HOLLYWOOD

Some racers Kitty knew had side jobs doing stunts for movie and TV actors that were too risky for the actors to do themselves. So Kitty decided to give stunt performing a try and ended up winning her greatest fame as a stuntperson! She crashed cars against trees and jumped off rooftops. She was burned, drowned, and dangled from airplanes in the sky. She raced motorcycles inside houses and dodged bullets. And she even fought off enemies, from robbers to wild animals, using knives, guns, and her fists!

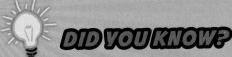

DID YOU KNOW?

Not everyone can become a stuntperson. You have to be fearless, fit, and willing to take dangerous risks as part of the job. You must also be skilled at driving and crashing cars and motorcycles; jumping from great heights; climbing mountains, buildings, and towers; and fighting with guns, swords, and fists. And you must do all this without getting hurt, or push through the pain if something does go wrong!

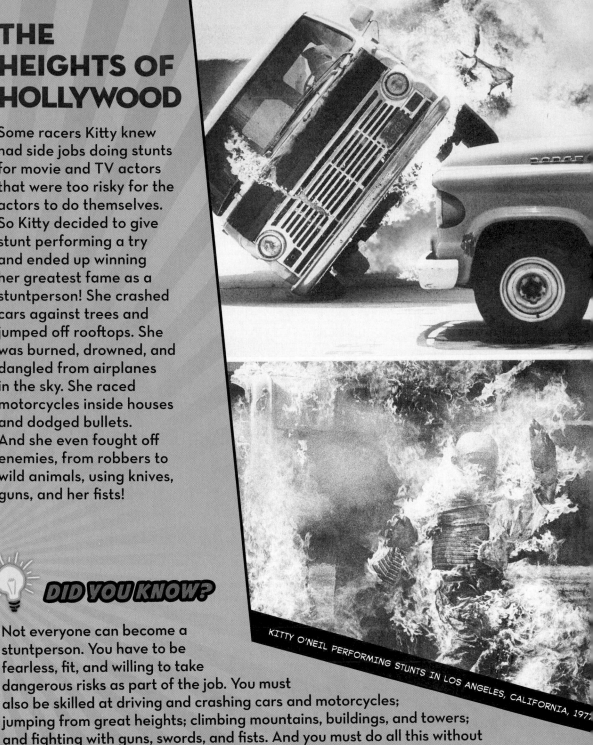

KITTY O'NEIL PERFORMING STUNTS IN LOS ANGELES, CALIFORNIA, 197?

STUNT 3 | VAN EXPLOSION!

In an early TV special, Kitty combined a high-speed, death-defying car chase with two other stunts. Here's what happened:

1 First, she drove a van at top speed down a busy street full of cars.

2 As the police gave chase, Kitty dashed in and out of lanes trying to escape.

3 From the middle lane, she made a sudden, sharp right turn, and cut off a car that crashed into a building!

4 Then, Kitty headed up a ramp in a seven-floor parking garage.

5 With the cops behind her, she zipped around the circular ramp to the roof level and barreled through a wooden barrier.

6 On the roof, a parked car barred her way. She swerved to avoid a collision, but her van sideswiped the parked car, rolled over, and exploded.

7 With her clothes on fire, she broke free of the van, ran to the edge of the roof, and jumped seven floors down to the street!

Science Revealed!

Want to know the science behind Kitty's death-defying van explosion? Here's the scoop:

☑ The van was specially prepared for the stunt. It had a strong roll bar so its body would not collapse when rolling over. Also, the gas tank held just enough fuel for the stunt, but not enough to start a big explosion or fire. Kitty's clothes were fireproof.

☑ Crew members with fire extinguishers hid nearby, ready to put out any blazes.

☑ Finally, there was a giant inflated airbag on the sidewalk to catch Kitty after she jumped.

FREE FALLING!

On February 12, 1979, Kitty had to do an especially challenging stunt in a TV show. She had to jump off the roof of a 127-foot-tall hotel! A jump from this height had never been tried before.

The day was clear and cold. Kitty checked the airbag that would catch her. Was it inflated to the right pressure? Was it in the right position? On the day of the jump she did two practice jumps from lower heights. Both went well. She was ready.

The actual jump was picture-perfect. She spread her arms straight out and locked her legs together. To the crowd on the ground she looked like a bird in the sky. Seconds later, she landed at the center of the huge airbag.

After this success, Kitty tried to set a new women's free-fall record. She went up 180 feet in a helicopter, almost the height of a 20-story building. Again, a perfect jump and landing that made history. She set a new woman's free-fall record of 180 feet—and was listed in the *Guinness Book of World Records.*

Very few stuntpeople ever set world records. Kitty O'Neil is special—she set three world records in her lifetime.

O'NEIL PERFORMING JUMPING FOR A TV SHOW, 1979

WHAT DO *YOU* THINK?

IS IT WRONG FOR STUNTPEOPLE TO REPLACE ACTORS FOR STUNTS? ARE STUNT PERFORMERS REALLY ACTORS? SHOULD THERE BE AN ACADEMY AWARD CATEGORY FOR STUNTPEOPLE?

T8 REBECCA RUSCH

> I DON'T QUIT. I BREAK DOWN AND FEEL PAIN LIKE EVERYONE ELSE, BUT I JUST DON'T QUIT.

BORN:
AUGUST 25, 1968,
AGUADILLA,
PUERTO RICO

CLAIM TO FAME:
ADVENTURE RACER

PRESENT HOME:
KETCHUM, IDAHO

BEFORE THE RACES...

Rebecca Rusch says that her career began with a tracksuit. The tracksuit belonged to her older sister, Sharon, who ran on their suburban high school track team. To get a tracksuit of her own, her sister advised her to join the cross-country team. So Rebecca signed up for track, and she succeeded at it beyond her biggest dreams. She won long-distance track races and even longer cross-country races. Her bedroom was soon crammed full of medals, trophies, and plaques. On her way to becoming a champion runner, Rebecca learned a few things about herself: She could push very hard to win. She had great endurance. And she could withstand a lot of pain and fatigue. For all these reasons, she earned the nickname "Queen of Pain." Her main ambition was to challenge herself and finish first. These strengths stayed with Rebecca for life. They made her a great athlete, but her adventures were just beginning . . .

17

FIRST RACE, FIRST PLACE

In 1997, Rebecca joined a team of three young men for an adventure race. The race began on a beach in Malibu, California. It was to last 24 hours—without stops or rest! Rebecca's team launched their kayaks into the huge, breaking waves of the Pacific Ocean. They were off to a good start, unlike some other teams that struggled to get their kayaks afloat.

DID YOU KNOW?

Adventure racing is a team sport that includes activities such as running, mountain biking, and kayaking or rafting. Usually, there are four or five members and the teams are co-ed. A race lasts anywhere from two hours to two weeks and takes place in an unmarked wilderness area. Racers can only use a map and a compass to find their way around. Very importantly, they get little sleep at night to have more time for running the race.

Rebecca and her team paddled furiously until midnight, when they reached land. With grit and determination, Rebecca left the kayak and was eager to get on her mountain bike. But first there was lots of exciting trekking and navigating through the mountains.

Once on her bike, the task was to ride to the top of a very steep hill. Off she went on the super-hard ascent. The climb took every bit of her strength and endurance. Rebecca was afraid that she couldn't make it on her own. But she forced herself to keep going. She counted her pedal strokes—ten more, another ten, one more ten. Then she looked ahead. The steep trail had flattened out. She was thrilled to see that she had reached the top of the mountain. And she had done it all on her own. She had not only survived the first adventure race of her life, but she had helped her team win first place!

Science Revealed!

Mountain bikes are bicycles designed for riding on unpaved surfaces. The bikes themselves are sturdier than other bikes. They also have wide, knobby tires for riding on sand or rocks, with especially strong brakes.

JOKE

HOW DID THE BARBER WIN THE ADVENTURE RACE?

HE TOOK A SHORT CUT.

315 MILES IN MOROCCO

One of Rebecca's most exciting and challenging races was in 1998 in Morocco. There were mountains as high as 13,000 feet, and there was desert, which shifted from over 90 degrees Fahrenheit (F) at the hottest time of the day to below freezing at night. Very low temperatures brought the danger of hypothermia, even the risk of potential death. This ultra-endurance adventure race lasted 11 days and covered 315 miles.

The first leg, on camels, knocked a number of teams out of the race, but Rebecca's team did well and arrived at the Atlantic Ocean's edge in good shape.

Rebecca and the others ran for a few miles to reach their kayaks for a 50-mile paddle on the open ocean. The ocean was far rougher than the racers had ever seen. Six-foot waves pummeled Rebecca's small, fragile kayak and posed a big challenge. To stop at all the necessary checkpoints meant navigating in and out to shore while battling powerful currents. The water temperature was 62 degrees F, and the wind and cold ocean spray made it even colder. For two whole days, Rebecca and the others endured these killing conditions.

The team hiked and climbed through 107 miles of rocks and sand. Each member carried a 40-pound backpack filled with supplies.

On day three, 63 miles of desert mountains lay before them. They walked on bleeding, blistered feet and used their hiking poles as crutches. After a few hours, they landed in a cold, dark canyon and went to sleep. In the morning, they discovered they had climbed the wrong mountain! After marching all that morning, they discovered they were lost again! This time a helicopter guided them to the next checkpoint. They used ropes to climb down, or rappel, 14 tall, sheer cliffs.

Having finally made it to the right destination, it was time for the horse-riding part of the race. Then came the 120-mile bike ride to the finish line.

Rebecca's team was almost last to arrive. But despite all the hardships, she viewed the race as one of the most rewarding experiences of her life.

STUNT 3
RIVERBOARDING DOWN THE COLORADO RIVER

In November 2001, Rebecca and two friends set off to do what no one had ever done before: riverboard down the 300 miles of the Colorado River in the Grand Canyon—without any backup or other help. It would soon be winter, but they believed they could withstand the freezing-cold waters and navigate the waves and jagged rocks.

So the adventure began! The friends donned wet suits, booties, and helmets. They slipped fins on their feet to manage the river currents. They wore life jackets for safety. And they packed shin guards, gloves, kneepads, thigh pads, and elbow pads to protect themselves from the river rocks. Each one lay belly-down on her board. They towed their food and camping gear on separate riverboards behind them. Then they pushed off the sand and into the river.

Close call followed close call as they shot down the river. Every night they pitched tents and slept on the banks of the river. After 19 difficult days, they reached the end of the course. They were bruised, aching, and totally exhausted—but very proud of themselves.

DID YOU KNOW?

Riverboarding is a sport—here's how it works: You lie on a plastic board (think bodyboard) in a river. Typically, riverboards are two feet wide and four feet long with handles on the sides. You paddle with your hands and wear fins on your feet for moving and steering. The sport started in the mid-1980s.

WHERE IS SHE NOW?

Rebecca Rusch completed one adventure race a year for the next 10 years in a row! Each time there was a big adventure race someplace in the United States, she drove there, if possible. All told, she did 15 races in 15 different countries.

Rebecca has raised more than $100,000 for bike-related charities. In 2017, she promoted a movie called *Blood Road*, which tells the story of her thrilling ride along the 1,200-mile Ho Chi Minh Trail in search of the spot where her father lost his life during the Vietnam War. As long as adventure calls, Rebecca Rusch will take on new challenges!

REBECCA RUSCH RIDING THE HO CHI MINH TRAIL IN VIETNAM, 2015

17 ANNIE TAYLOR

> I WOULD RATHER FACE A CANNON, KNOWING THAT I WOULD BE BLOWN TO PIECES, THAN GO OVER THE FALLS AGAIN.

Queen of The Mist

BORN:
OCTOBER 24, 1838,
AUBURN, NEW YORK

CLAIM TO FAME:
FIRST PERSON TO SURVIVE A PLUNGE
OVER NIAGARA FALLS IN A BARREL

DIED:
APRTL 29, 1921,
LOCKPORT, NEW YORK

BEFORE THE FALLS...

Annie was born in a small town near Niagara Falls. She was one of eight children, and when she was only 12 years old her father died. But he left enough money for the family to have a comfortable life. After high school, Annie entered college to study teaching. After a four-year teacher training course, she graduated with honors. Shortly after starting to teach at a local school, she suffered two tragedies—her infant child died, and her husband was killed in the Civil War. Now a widow, Taylor continued to teach, but she never earned much money. By the time she was 60 years old, Taylor was running very low on funds and began to think of ways to make money quickly.

No, Annie Taylor wasn't a typical daredevil. She didn't grow up dreaming of living dangerously, and she didn't always want to push herself to the limit. Taylor became a daredevil for one reason and one reason only: to make money!

HATCHING THE PLAN

Taylor knew Niagara Falls well since she had grown up nearby. The falls had become a popular tourist attraction. Many daredevil swimmers swam across the river that led to the falls, and tightrope walkers crossed the falls on ropes strung overhead. For this they got lots of money and attention.

So Taylor came up with a bold idea: She'd do something that hadn't been done before—she'd ride over Niagara Falls in a barrel!

DID YOU KNOW?

Niagara Falls is the point where the Niagara River drops down nearly 200 feet; about 3,000 tons of water flow over the falls every second. On the border of the United States and Canada, Niagara Falls consists of three separate waterfalls.

1 Horseshoe Falls: The largest and most powerful, this one is on the Canadian side of the border.

2 American Falls: These falls are smaller and are on the New York State side of the border.

STEP 2 — BUILDING THE BARREL

Once Taylor had the idea, there was no stopping her. She found a company that made barrels for pickles, and she ordered an especially big one to hold her short, plump body. The barrel was about four and a half feet tall and three feet wide. It was made of sturdy oak and iron, with mattress-like padding on the inside.

☑ Annie had leather straps attached to the sides to hold her steady.

☑ To be upright as much as possible, she had a 200-pound weight placed at the bottom. If the barrel tumbled over, the weight would prop it up.

☑ The barrel also had an air hole in the top and a cork to plug the hole.

Two days before Taylor went over the falls, workers tested the barrel to make sure it was watertight and strong enough to withstand the rushing water. They also placed a cat inside the barrel to be sure a living being could survive the ride. Both barrel and cat passed the tests. Annie Taylor was ready to go!

3 Bridal Veil Falls: These are also smaller and are also on the New York State side of the border.

The word "Niagara" is believed to come from the Iroquois word "onguiaahra," which translates as "The Strait" or "Thunder of Water." One-fifth of all the fresh water on Earth passes over Niagara Falls.

STEP 3   BARRELING OVER

The date was October 24, 1901. It was Annie Taylor's 63rd birthday. She was much older than most first-time daredevils but every bit as brave.

On the day of the historic ride, a small rowboat carrying Taylor left the dock. The barrel bobbed along behind the boat, attached by a short rope. The boat headed out to a tiny island about one mile up the fast-flowing Niagara River from the falls.

On the island, assistants strapped Taylor inside the barrel. She held on tightly to her small, good-luck, heart-shaped pillow. They sealed the air hole and used a bicycle pump to blow extra air into the barrel. Then they pushed the barrel into the water, sending it superfast toward the falls.

Thousands watched from the shores. Horrified, they saw the barrel bounce and spin toward the brink of Horseshoe Falls. It toppled over the edge and plunged straight down. Then it disappeared from sight in the gushing water.

After 20 minutes, someone spotted it at the base of the falls! Was Annie Taylor okay?

A rescue boat sped over. They caught the barrel and towed it to shore. Workers sawed off the top of the barrel—it was the only way to free the daring woman. The job took more than an hour, but she was finally out. Taylor was bruised and had a cut on her forehead. But she was the first to do this stunt and come out alive!

STEP 4   FAME AND RICHES! (RIGHT?)

After Taylor recovered from the cut and bruises she got on the ride, she was invited to speak at the World's Fair in Buffalo, New York. She appeared there with the barrel and the cat that survived the tests. Later she had a counter in a souvenir shop in the city of Niagara Falls, New York. Here she sold small copies of her barrel, photos and postcards of herself, and a small booklet about her amazing feat. Taylor also earned some money posing for photos with tourists. Soon, though, interest in Annie Taylor faded. Sadly, her daring scheme never brought her the fame and riches she had hoped for.

ANNIE TAYLOR ROWING TO HORSESHOE FALLS, 1901

DID YOU KNOW?

It is now against the law to try to ride over Niagara Falls. Survivors face arrest and stiff fines. In 1985, a daredevil went over the falls in a barrel wrapped in inner tubes from rubber tires. He was fined a total of $5,503!

THE BITTER END

Shortly after her successful adventure over the falls, Annie ran into some bad luck. Her manager disappeared with the barrel! Annie spent most of her meager savings searching for the missing barrel. Eventually, detectives found and returned it.

Taylor struggled on with little money, as she had done her whole life. In March 1921, she fell ill and was taken to a hospital. She died there, penniless, on April 29, 1921, at age 82. She was buried in the special "Stunters" section of Oakwood Cemetery in Niagara Falls, New York, alongside other Niagara daredevils. The tombstone reads: "Annie Edson Taylor, First to go over the Horseshoe Fall in a Barrel and Live, October 24, 1901."

COPYCATS!

Annie Taylor was not the last person to take a wild trip over Niagara Falls—she inspired a number of others to follow her example. Between 1901 and 2003, 15 copycats tried the stunt. Only 10 of them survived.

Among the best known are:

1. Bobby Leach went over the falls in July 1911. He survived, but died some years later after slipping on an orange peel.

2. Red Hill Jr. tried to ride the falls in August 1951 in a vehicle made of 14 truck tire inner tubes wrapped in canvas and a heavy net. He lost his life in the attempt.

3. Steven Trotter made a successful trip in August 1985 in a barrel wrapped in giant tire inner tubes.

4. Peter DeBernardi and Jeffrey Petkovich plunged over the falls in September 1989 in a vehicle that looked like a mini submarine.

5. Jesse Sharp took the ride in a kayak in June 1990 but died.

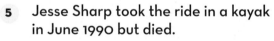

6. Robert Overacker used a Jet Ski in 1995 but his parachute didn't open and he was killed.

7. In October 2003, Kirk Jones was the first to ride the falls successfully in the clothes he was wearing and survived. In April 2017 he tried again, this time riding in a large inflated ball, but was killed.

16 CHARLES BLONDIN

> [A ROPEWALKER IS] LIKE A POET, BORN AND NOT MADE.

BORN:
FEBRUARY 24, 1824,
SAINT-OMER, FRANCE

CLAIM TO FAME:
WALKED MORE THAN
10,000 MILES ON TIGHTROPES

DIED:
FEBRUARY 22, 1897,
LONDON, ENGLAND

BECOMING "THE LITTLE WONDER"...

Charles Blondin was born as Jean-François Gravelet. He saw his first circus at the age of five and it made him want to try tightrope walking at home. He strung a clothesline between two kitchen chairs, placed them a few feet apart, and walked the rope. Not surprisingly, he fell off—but that would be his last fall.

Jean-François's father, a gymnast, was pleased to see his son's interest in tightrope walking. He enrolled five-year-old Jean-François in the French École de Gymnase, or School of Gymnastics. It was a great start to his life as a tightrope acrobat. Jean-François was an excellent student. He mastered walking on a tightrope fearlessly, without stumbling or falling. After only six months he was performing at events in his city of Lyon. He drew crowds at circuses and music halls throughout France and England. People praised his skill on the tightrope as well as his acting ability. By age eight, the show billed Jean-François as "The Little Wonder." And that was just the beginning . . .

STUNT 1 CROSSING THE FALLS

In 1858, Blondin (still Jean-François at the time), was touring with a group of acrobats, and they stopped at Niagara Falls. Blondin was awestruck. One year later, workers strung a rope 1,300 feet long and two inches wide from one side to the other. It was about 160 feet above the water—the height of a 16-story building. On June 30, 1859, some 25,000 thrill seekers lined both sides of Niagara Falls to witness this feat. Most people feared that Blondin would fall into the water and die.

DID YOU KNOW?

Jean-François changed his name to Charles Blondin when he became a professional tightrope walker. The new name came from his father's nickname, "Blondie," and from his own hair, which was pale yellow.

At exactly 4:45 p.m., Blondin stepped onto the rope. He wore pink tights covered with shimmering spangles and soft-soled shoes. He held a balancing pole that was 26 feet long and weighed 50 pounds.

Far below were the churning rapids of the Niagara River. Step by step, Blondin began to make his way from the American side to the Canadian side. He was about one-third of the way across when he plopped facedown on the cable. Uh-oh! The crowd was sure this was the end of Blondin!

But Blondin did not call for help. Instead, he lowered a long string to a little boat below, which was filled with viewers. The people attached a bottle of wine to the string. Blondin hauled it up and took a long drink. Then he stood up, waved to the cheering crowd, and continued until he arrived at the Canadian shore.

After a 20-minute rest on the Canadian side, Blondin started back on the tightrope. About 200 feet in, Blondin stopped and hooked his balancing pole onto the rope. Carefully, he unpacked the camera he had strapped to his back and snapped a picture of the crowd on the American side. Then he packed up and finished his walk. All in all, he made the round-trip crossing in 23 minutes.

"The Great Blondin" was cheered and celebrated. He was the first person to complete the most dangerous and deadly tightrope crossing over Niagara Falls.

Science Revealed!

The balancing pole is important to the safety of tightrope walkers because it gives them a way to improve their balance. The drooping ends of the pole lower the performers' center of gravity—the point at which they are perfectly balanced. The center of gravity is just below the belly button; the lower a person's center of gravity, the steadier the person.

STUNT 2

THE PIGGYBACK RIDE

One time, Blondin asked for a volunteer to be carried across on his back. His manager, Harry Colcord, reluctantly agreed. He climbed onto Blondin's back, wrapped his arms around Blondin's neck, and locked his legs around Blondin's waist. Blondin warned the frightened Colcord not to attempt to do any balancing on his own, otherwise they would both fall to their deaths!

The pair set out on the crossing. Six times Blondin seemed to make believe he was falling but regained his balance each time. The terrified Colcord held on for dear life as Blondin succeeded in bringing them safely to the other side.

STUNT 3

BREAKFAST ON THE ROPES

In his most famous act, Blondin carried a small iron stove, eggs, a plate, and a frying pan onto a rope over Niagara Falls. He walked to the rope's halfway point, stopped, and with a flourish started a fire in the stove. When it was ready, he cooked an omelet with the eggs and lowered the dish to passengers below on the *Maid of the Mist*. When done, Blondin calmly continued over the falls to the end of the rope.

CHARLES BLONDIN AND HARRY COLCOR CROSSING NIAGARA FALLS, 186

BLONDIN MAKING BREAKFAST OVE NIAGARA FALL

DID YOU KNOW?

Funambulist is a name sometimes given to tightrope walkers who do daring tricks and stunts on tightropes. The word combines funis, the Latin word for "rope," and ambulare, the Latin word for "walk."

KING OF THE FALLS

Blondin's high-wire acts over Niagara Falls continued to get more treacherous.

1. On July 4, only four days after his first trip, Blondin crossed again without his balancing pole. Halfway across, he lay down on the rope and flipped over. Then he walked backward to the opposite shore. For the return crossing he was blindfolded, with a thick, heavy sack over his head and body.

2. On July 15, he walked backward to Canada and forward to the United States pushing a wheelbarrow.

3. On July 29, he did backflips in both directions.

4. Blondin also crossed in the dark of night with locomotive headlights at either end lighting his way.

5. On another occasion, he struggled across with his body in chains.

BLONDIN UPSIDE DOWN OVER NIAGARA FALLS

JOKE

WHAT KIND OF MEAL DID BLONDIN COOK ON THE TIGHTROPE?

A WELL-BALANCED MEAL!

DEFYING DEATH!

According to some accounts, Blondin crossed Niagara Falls 300 times—each time more dangerous than the one before. Once, Blondin crossed the falls carrying a table and a chair. Just as he was about to sit down on the chair, the chair fell into the water! It was his closest near-death experience. Blondin wobbled a little but did not panic. He got his balance back. Then, looking cool—despite having just cheated death—Blondin sat down on the rope and ate a piece of cake at the table!

SUPER-TROUPER

After his run of Niagara Falls crossings, the fearless Blondin settled in England. Now very wealthy, he moved into a large house that he named Niagara Villa. He continued performing, mostly in England, but also in the United States and elsewhere. His last performance was in Ireland at age 72, and he died the following year.

YAKIMA CANUTT

BRONC RIDING AND BULLDOGGING WERE MY SPECIALTIES.

BORN:
NOVEMBER 29, 1895
(OR 1896), COLFAX,
WASHINGTON

CLAIM TO FAME:
WORLD'S CHAMPION ALL-ROUND COWBOY

DIED:
MAY 24, 1986,
NORTH HOLLYWOOD,
CALIFORNIA

BEFORE RODEO STARDOM...

Yakima Canutt was born on his family's ranch in Colfax, Washington. He rode his first bucking bronco at only 16 years of age. He climbed onto the saddle of a horse held inside a narrow pen called a "chute." A helper opened the gate and the horse burst out—kicking, jumping, and swinging from side to side. As the horse tried to throw him off, Canutt held on to the reins with one hand while keeping his other high in the air to steady himself. The young man had to stay on for at least eight seconds to qualify for a rodeo—and he did. Amazingly enough, only a year after his first rodeo, he won the title of World's Best Bronco Buster. Yakima's parents had actually named him Enos Edward Canutt. But, when he was about 19, a newspaper photographer snapped his picture while he was performing in a rodeo. Since Enos lived near Yakima Valley, the paper dubbed him Yakima Canutt. From then on, people called him Yak for short—a name by which he became a famous, award-winning cowboy and later, stuntman . . .

RIDE 'EM COWBOY

By 1923, Yak had already won the title of World's Champion All-Round Cowboy four times! So it was time for him to take on the greatest challenge for any bronco buster. He rode one of the most famous—and dangerous—of all bucking broncos, a horse named Tipperary. Some of the top rodeo cowboys had already tried to ride Tipperary, but this big, powerful horse threw every one of them to the ground. Only Yak met the challenge. He rode Tipperary twice and stayed in the saddle for the full eight seconds both times! After each ride, the crowd cheered this brave, daring young man.

JOKE

WHY ARE COWBOYS SO MUCH FUN?

THEY'RE ALWAYS HORSING AROUND?

DID YOU KNOW?

According to legend, Tipperary, the great bucking horse, got its name after it threw a cowboy to the ground. Sad and downhearted, the cowboy sat in the dust singing, "It's a Long Way to Tipperary," a popular song of the time. The horse's owner, hearing the song, decided to name the horse Tipperary. In 1979, long after its death, Tipperary the horse was elected to the ProRodeo Hall of Fame.

HOW TO BULLDOG A SPEEDING STEER

Yak wasn't just a fearless bronco buster—he was also a champion bulldogger! Bulldogging, or wrestling a steer to the ground, takes a lot of skill. Top rodeo cowboys like Yak could force a steer down in two or three seconds! Here's how Yak did it:

1 Galloping along at about 30 miles per hour, he guided his horse alongside the steer, leaned over, and grasped the steer's two horns.

2 As the steer tried to dash away, it pulled Yak off the horse's back.

3 As Yak fell, he twisted the steer's head with all his might.

4 Then, with a powerful thrust, the cowboy forced the steer's head down onto the ground.

5 As soon as all four of the steer's feet were in the air, an official waved a flag and the contest was over.

YAKIMA CANUTT BULLDOGGING AT THE RODEO, OREGON, 1912

SILVER SCREEN COWBOY

After years of starring in rodeos, and winning many championships and prizes, Yak launched a career in the movies. Hollywood directors hired him to be a stuntman in Western films. In 1939, Yak planned and performed one of the most famous stunts in the entire history of movies in *Stagecoach*.

In this film, a stagecoach speeds across a western landscape. From one side, a band of Apache Native American warriors thunders toward the coach. With a crack of the whip, the driver hurries the coach's horses on to escape. One Apache, played by Yak himself, breaks away from the group. He pulls ahead, bends low over the saddle, and spurs his horse to go faster and faster. The Apache gallops alongside the straining coach horses.

JOKE

"HAVE YOU EVER BEEN IN AN ACCIDENT?" THE NEWS REPORTER ASKED THE RODEO STAR.

"NO," SAID THE COWBOY.

"BUT YOU SAID YOU WERE THROWN BY A HORSE," THE REPORTER REPLIED.

"OH, THAT WAS NO ACCIDENT. THE HORSE DID IT ON PURPOSE!"

He leaps from his horse onto the neck of one of the horses pulling the coach. Then he flips backward over the horse and stands on the harness tongue—the long wooden bar that keeps the horses in their places. The guard on the coach fires his rifle. The bullet hits the Apache, who loses his footing and slips down under the harness tongue. The poor man holds on for dear life as the galloping horses drag him along the ground. Spooked by the gunshot, the horses run even faster and more furiously. The driver fires again. Once more, the bullet hits its mark. Badly wounded, the Apache loses his grip on the tongue and falls to the ground. The horses and coach sweep over him. This amazing stunt, which Yak both planned and carried out, made him the best-known of all Hollywood stuntmen.

DID YOU KNOW?

In 1981, stuntman Terry Leonard tried to repeat Yak's under-the-wagon stunt but was run over by the stagecoach and badly injured.

DAREDEVILS UNLIMITED

Twenty years after his great success with *Stagecoach*, Yak scored another incredible triumph in the film *Ben-Hur*. In this movie, his son, Joe, also a stuntman, followed in Yak's daring footsteps.

In *Ben-Hur*, Yak planned a nine-minute-long chariot race. For two years he trained horses to pull the chariots and taught actors and stuntmen to drive the chariots. Yak also worked out all the wrecks, crashes, turnovers, wheel locks, and skids that added excitement to the race—often performing the most dangerous, death-defying stunts himself. At one point, the movie's hero is racing around the track when he comes upon the wreck of a crashed chariot. Unable to avoid a collision, he passes over the wreckage. Yak's son, Joe, took over for the actor in this scene. He presses the chariot on very fast and barely makes it over the debris. His chariot bounces high up in the air. When it lands, the force propels Joe forward and out of the chariot. He comes down in between the carriage and the running horses. But he manages to hold on to the chariot, climb back in, finish the race, and even win!

STILL PHOTO FROM THE MOVIE *BEN-HUR*, 1959

14 RICHARD HALLIBURTON

> DREAMS COME TRUE. MINE DID, AND IT WAS AS COLORFUL AND SATISFYING AS ALL MY FLIGHTS OF FANCY HAD IMAGINED IT WOULD BE.

BORN:
JANUARY 9, 1900,
BROWNSVILLE,
TENNESSEE

CLAIM TO FAME:
WORLD ADVENTURER

DIED:
MARCH 24, 1939,
DISAPPEARED IN THE
PACIFIC OCEAN

BEFORE HE DARED...

Richard Halliburton was born in a small Tennessee town. He was a sickly child but active and adventuresome. Even his mother remarked that as a young boy, the most dangerous things always appealed to him. Richard had many childhood friends, but his favorite playmates were a pet pony and a pet dog. One day he fell off the pony and was dragged on the ground. To everyone's surprise Richard didn't cry or seem frightened. At an early age he was sent to boarding school; college followed. In 1921, after he graduated, he left school for good. He yearned for adventures in the farthest corners of Earth, and he would spend the rest of his life chasing them...

The Matterhorn is considered one of the most dangerous mountains in the world. In 1865, seven climbers from England were the first to reach the summit. But climbing down, four of the seven plunged to their deaths. Since then, more than 500 climbers have died trying to conquer the Matterhorn.

STUNT 1

The Matterhorn is a very tall mountain on the border between Switzerland and Italy. Its snow-covered peak rises nearly three miles in the air. From its base, it looks like a pyramid with steep, sloping walls of rock and ice.

Halliburton began his climb at dawn on September 24, 1921. A friend and two guides joined him. The temperature was near zero degrees F. The winds were howling. The falling snow stung their faces.

The hardest part of the climb was near the peak. A rocky ledge jutted straight out from the face of the mountain. The guide, who was already on the ledge, lowered a rope for Halliburton. Halliburton struggled to rise, but about halfway up, his muscles gave out. All he could do was cling desperately to the rope as the guide hoisted him up.

Exhausted as he was, Halliburton kept climbing. Finally, he reached the summit. As he later wrote to his father, this was an experience he felt he might never match!

DEFYING DEATH!

One time while climbing the Matterhorn, Halliburton lost his balance and grabbed on to the mountainside. But the stone he grabbed on to broke loose! His boots slipped and he started to fall. Snow and rocks tumbled down the mountain as he struggled to right himself. Halliburton's guide tugged on the long rope between them and pulled him back against the mountain. Halliburton placed his boot in a crack in the ice and steadied himself. Phew!

SWIMMING THE PANAMA CANAL

Halliburton dared himself to swim the 51-mile-long Panama Canal, the body of water that links the Atlantic and Pacific Oceans. But he faced problems. First, there were many flesh-eating crocodiles and barracuda fish in the canal waters. Second, only ships, not people, were allowed to pass through the canal.

So Halliburton hired a sharpshooter, or a person who is skilled at shooting a gun, to row alongside him for protection. And he registered himself as a "ship," the SS *Halliburton*! The fee for going through the Panama Canal is based on a ship's weight. Since the "SS *Halliburton*" weighed about 140 pounds, he paid only 36 cents! Halliburton swam every day and went ashore at night. One day, he swam through a powerful rainstorm that made swimming very slow and difficult. Near the end of the swim, the sharpshooter spotted a school of barracudas and pulled Halliburton into the rowboat until it was safe again. It took Halliburton 10 days to swim from the Atlantic to the Pacific Ocean. At the end, he had painful blisters on his back from severe sunburn, and he was running a high fever. But despite his ailments, he began planning his next adventure without any delay!

DEFYING DEATH—AGAIN!

One day during his Panama Canal swim, a giant ship loomed above Halliburton. He felt the vibration of its engines and the pull of its propellers. There was little he could do to get out of its way. As the ship sailed along, the spinning propellers drew Halliburton closer and closer. But just as he was about to give up the fight, the ship began to turn. He was free from danger!

RICHARD HALLIBURTON (RIGHT) AND MOYE STEPHENS WITH *THE FLYING CARPET*, 1931

STUNT 3

In 1930, Halliburton wanted an even riskier adventure. His goal was to take an aerial photo of Mount Everest, which is 29,029 feet (5.5 miles) at its peak, according to the most recent measurement, and is the tallest mountain in the world. Halliburton wanted to do this from a height of about 18,000 feet (3.4 miles). The only way was from an airplane.

So Halliburton bought a plane—*The Flying Carpet*—and hired Moye Stephens, an experienced stunt pilot, to fly it. Unfortunately, the highest altitude his plane could reach was 16,000 feet (3 miles). What to do? Halliburton urged Stephens to try for 18,000 feet. As the plane rose toward the peak, Halliburton and Stephens gasped for breath. The air was thin and they suffered blasts of cold wind from the mountain. Despite fur-lined suits and gloves, their bodies became numb. It was a risky move, but Halliburton finally got his photo finish. And it was the very first aerial photo of Mount Everest!

DEFYING DEATH—THE FINAL GETAWAY

Halliburton's photograph of Mount Everest almost didn't happen. As the plane reached 18,000 feet, it struggled to fly in the cold, thin air. Stephens wanted to turn back, but Halliburton was determined to get his picture. He stood up, aimed his camera at the mountain, and clicked. But standing up shifted the plane's center of gravity. It also blocked the flow of air over the plane. The engine sputtered and stopped! The plane plunged, nose first. Halliburton dropped into his seat as Stephens struggled to restart the engine. The plane was heading straight for the side of the mountain. Finally, there was a loud roar. The engine turned over and the propeller began spinning. Slowly, *The Flying Carpet* started to rise. Halliburton and Stephens were safe, but nearly died trying!

WHAT DO *YOU* THINK?

TWO MAJOR EVENTS OCCURRED IN 1920: THE UNITED STATES RATIFIED THE NINETEENTH AMENDMENT TO THE CONSTITUTION, GIVING WOMEN THE RIGHT TO VOTE. AND THE FIRST BROADCAST OF VOICE AND MUSIC BEGAN OVER EARLY RADIO STATIONS. HOW DID THESE TWO MAJOR EVENTS CHANGE LIFE IN AMERICA?

A friend gave Halliburton an idea for what proved to be his last daredevil adventure: to sail across the Pacific Ocean from China to California. The plan was to arrive in time for the opening of the 1939 Golden Gate International Exposition in San Francisco.

Halliburton ordered a Chinese junk, a type of small, wooden boat, to be built for the voyage. He named it the *Sea Dragon* and set sail on March 4, 1939. On March 13 and 19, the captain on board radioed that all was well. But on the 23rd, the message was far more ominous. The junk reported strong winds, heavy rain, and high seas. Forty-foot waves smashed against the boat. The next morning, the ship's deck was underwater. The captain's message ended with a touch of humor: "Having wonderful time. Wish you were here instead of me." After that, silence.

US Navy ships and planes searched for the *Sea Dragon* and its crew. But they found nothing. After defying death again and again, Halliburton had run out of luck. Halliburton and his crew were presumed to have died at sea on March 24, 1939.

HALLIBURTON WITH THE CHINESE JUNK *SEA DRAGON*

THE HALLIBURTON LEGACY

In addition to these daring stunts, Halliburton also dove into the Mexican Well of Death, visited headhunters in Borneo, rode an elephant across the Alps, slept atop an Egyptian pyramid, was captured by pirates, and was imprisoned on Devil's Island! His legacy goes on in the books he wrote about his adventures: climbing the Matterhorn in *The Royal Road to Romance*, swimming the Panama Canal in *New Worlds to Conquer*, and photographing Mount Everest in *The Flying Carpet*.

13 JEB CORLISS

IF THIS DOESN'T SCARE YOU, I DON'T KNOW WHAT DOES.

BORN:
MARCH 25, 1976,
SANTA FE, NEW
MEXICO

CLAIM TO FAME:
PROFESSIONAL
BASE JUMPER

PRESENT HOME:
VENICE, CALIFORNIA

BEFORE THE JUMPS...

Jeb Corliss's parents made a living selling art objects from around the world. They often took Jeb and his two sisters on globe-trotting trips, buying pieces for their business. By the time he was six years old, Jeb had lived in five countries! Jeb attended school in the United States, but his family stayed on the move. He made few friends because he was always the new kid in school. In one desert home, his hobby was capturing rattlesnakes and poisonous spiders. To him, they were pets and playmates. He recalls sitting in his aunt's car watching birds soaring in the air and remarking to her that he, too, would fly one day. And he did! Corliss saw his first BASE jumper on TV when he was about 16. The man stood at the edge of a cliff, jumped off, and landed safely under his parachute. Corliss was thunderstruck! He made up his mind to become a BASE jumper.

The word BASE is an acronym. The letters B, A, S, E stand for the four different locations from which jumpers may start their jump: B for buildings, A for antennae, S for spans (or bridges), and E for earth (or cliffs). BASE jumpers leap from great heights and head down in free fall. As BASE jumpers get close to the ground, they open parachutes and float gently down to a landing. BASE jumping is considered one of the most dangerous and life-threatening of all adventure sports.

DEFYING DEATH

At 23, only one year after Corliss began training, he jumped over the very tall Howick Falls in South Africa—and almost plummeted to his death! He jumped off a ledge near the falls, and the waterfall sucked him in and collapsed his parachute. While tumbling down the falls, Corliss slammed into two rocky ledges. When he reached the bottom, the rushing water pushed Corliss to shore, but he wasn't able to pull himself onto land. He waited in the freezing water for about an hour before a friend rescued him, and another two hours for an ambulance to take him to a hospital. He broke his back in three places, fractured his left foot, chipped a tooth, tore his skin, and cracked a few ribs. Corliss soon realized that he had to wise up and master BASE jumping or his next jump might be his last!

WINGSUIT JUMPING OFF THE MATTERHORN

Some BASE jumpers wear wingsuits for their thrilling and deadly jumps. Wingsuits cover the entire body just like wet suits, but they have fabric between the wearers' arms, sides, and legs, making jumpers look like huge flying squirrels. With wingsuits, fliers can reach speeds of 120 miles an hour! This makes it incredibly dangerous—so dangerous that wingsuit jumping is illegal in almost every city in the United States and its national parks. But wingsuit jumping is legal in Europe, so Corliss went there to fly down a side of the Matterhorn, one of the tallest mountains in Europe. In September 2009, a helicopter flew a wingsuited Corliss to a point above the peak of the mountain. Corliss jumped, facedown, with his arms and legs spread apart. He whizzed down at a height of between five and ten feet above the icy surface—but he landed safely.

Science Revealed!

BASE jumpers use parachutes to slow their fall from a great height. Gravity pulls the jumper down toward the earth, while air caught in the parachute slows down the jumper's fall. Because gravity is stronger than the slowdown, or resistance, the jumper continues to fall, but more slowly.

JOKE!

WHAT LAW IS MOST IMPORTANT TO BASE JUMPERS?

THE LAW OF GRAVITY.

THE FLYING DAGGER

JUMP 2

In September 2013, Corliss planned to jump from a helicopter through a narrow crack in China's Langshan Mountain. The V-shaped opening is 60 feet wide at the top but only 15 feet wide at the bottom. It was like putting a thread through the small hole in a needle. But there was one big difference: a miss of only a few feet would mean certain death.

On the day of the event, 2,000 crew members, 90 search-and-rescue staff, thousands of spectators on the ground, and 350 million TV watchers stood by for the jump. Corliss, wearing his wingsuit, took off in the helicopter. As the helicopter passed over the crack, Corliss jumped and swept down into the 300-foot-long crack at an insane 122 miles an hour! The ride down was bumpy. The winds were whipping around the mountain. Corliss aimed his body at the tiny opening, desperately trying to avoid slamming into the stone walls on both sides. It took just five seconds to reach the other side—and to open the parachute. Corliss had just made the most terrifying jump of his life, and perhaps the riskiest wingsuit jump of all time. After all, with a name like "The Flying Dagger," who could beat it?

JEB CORLISS BASE JUMPING THROUGH LANGSHAN MOUNTAIN, 2013

DID YOU KNOW?

Wingsuit jumping is an expensive sport! Brand-new, made-to-order wingsuits can cost as much as $2,500. Most are nylon, but they can also be other fabrics. Of course, wingsuits that are specially made for Jeb Corliss and other professionals cost far more.

DEFYING THE LAW

Like all BASE jumpers, Corliss dreamed of jumping from the top of the Empire State Building to the streets of New York City. But the building's guards watched out for jumpers like him. On the day of his planned jump, he tried to trick the guards by wearing a fat suit to make him look chubby, with gray hair and a beard to look old. He took the elevator up to the observation deck on the 86th floor and all looked clear. He changed his outfit quickly, walked over to the tall steel fence, and started to scale it. Several guards saw him, yanked him back over the fence, and turned him over to the police. There was a trial and the judge passed sentence: Corliss would never be allowed into the Empire State Building again!

DEFYING DEATH—AGAIN!

Corliss almost leaped to his death wingsuit jumping from the peak of Table Mountain in South Africa. As he sped down the mountainside at about 120 miles per hour, Corliss's left foot clipped the side of a big boulder. The snag tipped him forward, and he crashed into the side of the mountain! Corliss escaped with a broken leg, a torn ligament, three broken toes, and large gashes in his skin. He was airlifted and taken to a hospital. It took over a year for Corliss to recover completely.

THE HUMAN ARROW

For his wingsuit jump in May 2016, Corliss aimed his body at a target: a small black bull's-eye about the size of an apple. The stunt was called "The Human Arrow," and the event was held at the Great Wall of China. A big, white, paper banner was stretched between two poles above the wall. Right in the center of the banner was the target bull's-eye. Corliss jumped from a helicopter 6,000 feet in the air. He flew toward the target at a speed of 120 miles per hour. The human arrow scored a perfect bull's-eye! His head went right through the center of the bull's-eye, ripping the paper in half. The torn paper banner fluttered in the wind as he continued his flight. Then, Corliss opened the parachute and gently floated to the ground. The TV cameras on Corliss's helmet captured the entire jump and it was livestreamed to thousands around the world.

WHAT DO YOU THINK?
SHOULD WINGSUIT JUMPING BE MADE LEGAL THROUGHOUT THE UNITED STATES? SHOULD THE GOVERNMENT STOP ANY ADULT WHO IS WILLING TO TRY? DOES WINGSUIT JUMPING HARM ANYONE BUT THE JUMPER?

12 AUGUSTE PICCARD

> IF YOU WANT TO GO INTO UNKNOWN TERRITORY, TO SOMEWHERE NO ONE HAS BEEN BEFORE, YOU JUST INVENT A DEVICE TO DO IT, AND OFF YOU GO.

BORN:
JANUARY 28, 1884,
BASEL, SWITZERLAND

CLAIM TO FAME:
FIRST TO FLY HIGHER AND DIVE DEEPER
THAN ANYONE ELSE IN THE WORLD

DIED:
MARCH 24, 1962,
LAUSANNE, SWITZERLAND

BEFORE TESTING THE LIMITS...

Auguste Piccard and Jean-Felix were identical twins whom even their mother had a hard time telling apart. Their father taught chemistry at a Swiss university and, not surprisingly, Auguste and Jean-Felix grew up very science-minded. Experimenting with heat and electricity was a favorite hobby. At age 14, the boys saw a hot-air balloon show. Young as they were, they set out to fly their own hot-air balloon. Their first experiment failed when the balloon caught fire. Yet, it started Auguste thinking about building a balloon able to carry him up to the stratosphere, the layer of air from 6 to 30 miles above the ground. At the same time, the boys read popular science fiction novels by Jules Verne. One told of a sea captain who explored the world's oceans in a submarine where he saw monsters and strange fish that lived on the ocean bottom. Such stories led Auguste, especially, to dream of building a submarine that could actually take him to the oceans' lowest depths. Little did he know that he would spend a lifetime realizing these two wild dreams!

THE HIGH-ALTITUDE BALLOON

In 1913, more than 10 years after the brothers built their first balloon, Auguste was studying cosmic rays while teaching physics at a university. He wondered: could he design a balloon to carry him up into Earth's stratosphere and help him study cosmic rays?

Would it be able to rise and then come down for a safe landing? How would he breathe at the very low pressure at that height? Was he brave enough to go into unknown space? For the next 10 years, Piccard worked out answers to these questions. Finally, in 1930, he invented a balloon that could rise higher than any balloon of the time. It was built like a huge ball and filled with hydrogen—a gas that is much lighter than air. Piccard attached a hollow, seven-foot-wide, airtight cabin to the bottom of the ball. Inside, there was room for two people. He called the cabin a gondola.

The hydrogen-filled balloon carried the gondola into the stratosphere. A pump raised the pressure and added oxygen to the air inside the gondola. Travelers could breathe just as they did on Earth's surface! Piccard put his own life on the line for science. Now he made plans to go up in the balloon himself!

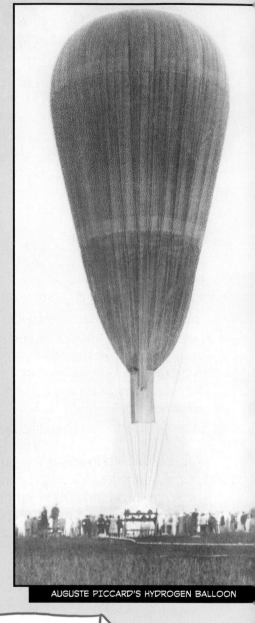

AUGUSTE PICCARD'S HYDROGEN BALLOON

Science Revealed!

Cosmic rays are forms of energy that travel to Earth from the sun, stars, and galaxies. But as they come close to Earth they are changed by Earth's atmosphere. Studying cosmic rays before they reach Earth's atmosphere would tell Piccard more about the rays.

UP, UP, AND AWAY

The launch date for Piccard's balloon and gondola adventure was May 27, 1931. Piccard and his assistant, Charles Kipfer, climbed inside the gondola. Days before the flight, government officials insisted the men wear helmets. But helmets were not available. So Mrs. Piccard took two small breadbaskets, stuffed each with a pillow, and produced two very peculiar head protectors!

The flight had a rough start. For one thing, the balloon had lifted up without warning! It didn't take long for the men to notice other problems: a whistling sound as air escaped from a leak in the gondola (Piccard quickly plugged it with some Vaseline and cotton); a motor overheated and temperatures in the cabin rose to 100 degrees F; and a valve broke preventing a smooth landing. But overall, the trip was a huge success. The flight lasted 17 hours, and the adventurers landed safely on a mountaintop in Austria with just one hour's worth of oxygen left!

The brave and brilliant Piccard had flown nearly 10 miles, 51,775 feet, above Earth—shattering every aircraft record. He brought back a huge amount of data on cosmic rays and conditions in the upper atmosphere. And he paved the way for future—and much higher—flights into space. He became the first person ever to see the curvature of Earth with his own eyes. A few years later, his research made it possible for Piccard's brother, Jean-Felix, and his wife, Jeannette, to reach 57,579 feet in their 1934 flight—more than a mile higher than Auguste's first flight.

JOKE

WHAT MUSIC DO YOU NOT WANT TO HEAR WHILE BEING CARRIED BY A BALLOON?

"POP" MUSIC!

 DID YOU KNOW?

Airliners today can fly very high in Earth's atmosphere. They all have pressurized cabins, thanks to Piccard's gondola invention.

THE BATHYSCAPHE

After his flight into space, Piccard turned his mind in another direction: to the deep ocean bottom. At that time, ocean exploration was done by submarine or in a cabin lowered at the end of a long rope. But that limited the depth of the dive, and Piccard wanted to go much deeper than a rope would let him. Could a balloon lower and raise him in the water, he wondered?

After much hard work, Piccard invented a huge, two-part diving vessel called a bathyscaphe. The larger top part, called the float, acts like the balloon. It lowers the bathyscaphe and brings it back up to the surface. Atop the cigar-shaped float, two propellers propel the bathyscaphe. Attached to the bottom of the float is a small cabin with room for passengers. The cabin has thick steel walls to withstand the tremendous water pressure at the bottom of the sea.

Piccard took several dives with the first bathyscaphe. Then, helped by his son, Jacques, he built a better, more modern bathyscaphe. They named it *Trieste*.

INTERIOR OF PICCARD'S BATHYSCAPHE

DOWN, DOWN, AND INTO THE DEEP

In August 1953, Auguste and Jacques tested the *Trieste* in a dive in the Mediterranean Sea off the coast of Italy. They dropped to a depth of nearly two miles. Although they heard frightening, crackling noises on the way down, they safely made the journey there and back. That same year the US Navy bought and improved the *Trieste* so that it could reach even lower depths.

EXTERIOR OF PICCARD'S BATHYSCAPHE

 ## Science Revealed!

The term bathyscaphe comes from the Greek words for "deep boat." In the bathyscaphe, the float contains large tanks filled with thousands of gallons of gasoline—enough to drive a car around Earth 25 times. Gasoline, which is lighter than water, helps raise the float in the water. The gasoline tanks are sealed shut. Workers fill other tanks with air when the float is on the surface. To go down, they allow seawater to flow into the tanks and the float slowly descends. Tons of small iron balls fill two other tanks. To rise, they drop the balls into the ocean. This cuts the weight and lets the bathyscaphe float up to the surface.

EXPEDITION 3

TO THE DEEPEST OCEAN BOTTOM

On January 23, 1960, Auguste Piccard watched his son and two others take the *Trieste* on a record-breaking dive in the western Pacific Ocean. They went down seven miles into the Mariana Trench, the lowest, deepest point on planet Earth! If you put Mount Everest, the world's highest mountain, at the bottom of the underwater Mariana Trench, the top of Mount Everest would be about a mile below the ocean surface. With Piccard's *Trieste* dive, the three men set a world record that has not yet been broken.

From the *Trieste*, the crew saw fish, shrimp, and other marine life floating by the porthole! It was a huge surprise. No one had expected to find so many living creatures at this great depth. The discovery would later lead to a ban on the dumping of nuclear waste at sea.

DID YOU KNOW?

The daredevil gene that passed from Auguste Piccard to his son, Jacques, passed to his grandson Bertrand. He made the first nonstop, round-the-world balloon flight in 1999. The trip took only 19 days!

11 NIK WALLENDA

> WALKING THE WIRE TO ME IS LIFE. . . . IT'S WHAT I LOVE TO DO

BORN:
JANUARY 24, 1979,
SARASOTA, FLORIDA

CLAIM TO FAME:
NINE-TIME HIGH-WIRE
WORLD RECORD HOLDER

PRESENT HOME:
SARASOTA, FLORIDA

BEFORE HE BROKE WORLD RECORDS...

Both of Nik Wallenda's parents were circus performers. They were part of the "Great Wallendas," a family of acrobats and high-wire walkers that goes back seven generations. Nik watched his parents practice and was eager to try. When Nik was just two years old, his parents set up a child-size high wire just a couple of feet above the ground. At first Nik tried, fell, got up, and fell again. But he persisted. Soon he was able to walk the entire length of the wire without falling. As a little boy, Nik performed in the circus alongside his grandfather, Alberto Zoppe. When he was 13, Nik did his first high-wire act—30 feet above the ground. And by 18, he performed the most dangerous of all high-wire stunts—the Human Pyramid. Walking the high wire was in Nik's blood, and this was just the beginning . . .

ACT 1 A FAMILY AFFAIR

The most famous Wallenda family act was the seven-person Human Pyramid. In March 1998, Nik, his father, and two other Wallendas formed the base of the pyramid. The front two rested a long bar on their shoulders. The back two did the same. The next level had one person standing on each bar. They held a bar between them. Balanced on this bar was the seventh person, Nik's mother, seated in a chair. The whole pyramid moved slowly across the wire. Halfway across, Mom stood up on the seat of her chair. The audience gasped. Then she sat down, and the pyramid of Wallendas walked to the end of the wire. The stunt worked perfectly. Nik felt so proud.

When Nik was only 21 years old, he had an even bolder idea: the family would make a four-level, eight-person pyramid, with another family member sitting on his mother's shoulders at the very top! They first performed this death-defying act at an amusement park in Kurashiki, Japan. The event earned a place in the *Guinness Book of World Records* as the tallest tightrope human pyramid ever attempted!

DID YOU KNOW?

High-wire walkers wear special shoes made of very soft leather. Nik's mother made his shoes out of cowhide or suede, as well.

WHEELS ON A WIRE

On October 15, 2008, Nik's high-wire act was broadcast on TV's *Today* show as he attempted one of his most dangerous feats yet—crossing the high wire on a bicycle! The steel wire was 135 feet high—and 235 feet long. It was less than an inch thick—about the diameter of a nickel. In his hands he carried his 45-pound balancing pole.

In the first part of his stunt, he walked about halfway across the wire. A fall from this height would mean instant death. Nevertheless, Wallenda boldly sat down on the wire and phoned the show's hosts on air! The call done, Nik resumed his walk and arrived at the other end of the wire safely.

For his return trip, Nik got on the same high wire riding a bicycle. He had removed the handlebars and the tires, so the frame of the wheels sat on the wire, much like a train on a track. Nik had almost arrived at the other end when he felt the back wheel lock and the bike slip backward. He was in touch with his father through a headset, and heard his father yell, "Don't back up!" The bike tottered and for the first time in his life, Nik wondered if he was about to fall. But he didn't lose his cool. He let the bike roll backward for a few seconds before gently pressing on the pedals. Slowly, the shaky bike inched forward. Bit by bit, Nik reached the end of the wire, where his wife and children greeted him with kisses and big bear hugs. The bike act set the Guinness World Record for longest bike ride on a high wire.

NIK WALLENDA BIKING ACROSS THE WIRE, NEW JERSEY, 2008

DEFYING DEATH

In 2011, Nik performed two death-defying acts high in the air. First, he flew up in a helicopter, climbed out, and worked his way down two ropes that held a trapeze. Then, he did the most extraordinary thing. He hung upside down from the trapeze for several seconds, holding on only with his toes! For the second helicopter stunt, he attached a special mouthpiece to the trapeze. He got out of the plane, moved down the ropes, and grasped the mouthpiece with his teeth. Incredible! He hung there for a short while, before clambering back into the helicopter.

ACT 3
CROSSING THE CANYON

In 2013, Nik lived out another dream—he became the first person to cross the Grand Canyon on a high wire. From the first time he visited the Grand Canyon as a teenager, he had the desire to cross it. He was not allowed to perform inside the Grand Canyon National Park. So Nik chose a section of the Grand Canyon a little farther east and outside the park, but on land belonging to the Navajo Nation. Nik's wire stretched nearly a quarter of a mile across the canyon.

The temperature that day was a warm 84 degrees F. But there were strong gusts of wind, some as fast as 48 miles per hour. The wind made the wire bounce. After about 13 minutes, Nik stopped and sat down to steady himself and control the bouncing. He then resumed the walk. It took him more than 22 minutes to get across. A happy man, he jogged and hopped the last few steps! TV stations in 217 countries around the world telecast Nik's Grand Canyon walk live. But they had a 10-second delay—just in case of an accident.

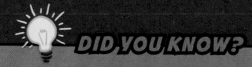

DID YOU KNOW?

The two sides of the Grand Canyon rise more than a mile above the Colorado River flowing at the bottom. The north rim is slightly higher than the south rim.

WALLENDA CROSSING THE GRAND CANYON, 2013

DID YOU KNOW?

When walking on a high wire, the wire sometimes begins to sway in rhythm. So Nik always changes the speed of his steps to avoid the sway.

 **ACT 4** # RAISING THE STAKES

Nik Wallenda will never forget the evening of November 2, 2014, in Chicago. After sundown, he broke two all-time world records.

His first walk started at a height of 588 feet on Marina City's west tower. From there he walked up over the Chicago River at a steep 19-degree angle to a height of 671 feet on the Leo Burnett Building. The quarter-of-a-mile-long tightrope was painted white to make it visible in the dark. The perilous crossing took about seven minutes. It broke the world record for the steepest tightrope walk between two buildings.

Nik's second Chicago walk occurred later the same day on a tightrope between Marina City's west tower and its twin, Marina City's east tower. The tightrope between the two towers stretched 94 feet, the length of a professional basketball court, at a height of 543 feet. But this time, the fearless daredevil went the distance wearing a blindfold! It took Nik 75 seconds to cross over. With that he broke still another world record. This time it was for the highest blindfolded tightrope walk! What a day it was!

DID YOU KNOW?

The blindfolded walk was so dangerous that Nik asked onlookers to be silent. He needed to concentrate without distraction.

WALLENDA CROSSING THE CHICAGO RIVER, 2014

10 ALAIN ROBERT

> MAN CREATES HIS OWN LIMITS, BUT WE ALL HAVE IN US THE POWER TO OVERCOME THEM AND TO REACH OUR GOALS.

BORN:
AUGUST 7, 1962,
BOURGOGNE, FRANCE

CLAIM TO FAME:
EXTREME CLIMBER

PRESENT HOME:
PÉZENAS, FRANCE

BEFORE HE WAS SPIDERMAN . . .

As a boy, Alain Robert was afraid of everything—including heights. But that all changed when he was nine years old and he saw a movie called *The Mountain*. It told the story of two mountain climbers who rescued a survivor of a plane crash on a mountaintop. The movie inspired Alain to be as fearless as the climbers in the film. Alain became a Cub Scout and learned to climb rocks. At age 12, he got the chance to try out his new skill when he arrived at his family's seventh floor apartment one day without his keys. His parents would not be home for several hours. Recklessly, Alain climbed up the outside wall of the apartment! When he reached the seventh floor, he entered the apartment through an unlocked window. So began Alain's life of climbing . . .

SCIENCE REVEALED!

Just like a scientist, Robert carefully examines the buildings he's planning to climb. He looks for spaces or cracks between the bricks or stones that he can grab to pull himself up. He pays particular attention to windows, metal bars or edges, and ledges and ridges. Always very well prepared, he climbs without a net, rope, harness, or any other safety device.

 **STUNT 1** ## BECOMING SPIDERMAN

In 1994, a film director telephoned Alain, who had already gained fame as a mountain climber. Could Alain come to Chicago and climb the 40-story Citibank Citicorp Center (now known as Citigroup Center) building for an upcoming film? Sure, why not!

When Alain arrived, however, there was a hitch. The film company had not obtained permission for the climb. Without permission, Alain guessed that the police and firefighters would try to stop him at the outset. But he knew that the fire department ladders could not reach very high. So, he hatched a plan: he would race up the first few stories on the building, and then climb the remaining 38 floors of the building at his usual speed. Nevertheless, when he arrived at the top, there were cops waiting to arrest him. They rushed him off to a police station, but only kept him there for a few hours. Years later Alain said the climb had changed his life. He had a new career as a real-life Spiderman!

SPIDERMAN ATOP THE EIFFEL TOWER

STUNT 2

The Eiffel Tower, a huge iron tower in Paris, opened in 1889. For 41 years it was the tallest structure in the world. Alain arrived at the tower late at night on December 31, 1996. The weather was freezing cold, and ice and snow covered the ground and the tower's steel beams. Alain wore warm trousers, a fur-lined jacket, an overcoat on top of it, and two pairs of gloves to stave off the cold.

Alain began his illegal climb in the hope of reaching the top without being stopped. But the guards spotted him as soon as he passed the first floor. They shouted at him to come down, and he shouted back that he intended to finish his climb. So the guards gave chase and tried to grab him on the second floor. He edged toward them—then darted away, teasing that he'd see them up on the third floor. Alain kept going and going until he reached the tower's top, 984 feet in the air. The climb up took him 45 minutes. The police were waiting for him at the top. They took him to the police station. But it was a holiday, and luckily for him, the officers weren't in the mood to arrest anyone. So they sent him home. Happy New Year!

DEFYING DEATH

In 1982, at age 20, Alain fell from a high cliff and crashed down nearly 50 feet, just narrowly escaping death! He landed headfirst, was knocked unconscious, and shattered his body on the jagged rocks. Two years of rehabilitation and therapy followed. Finally, he recovered, but he would suffer from vertigo, a type of dizziness or feeling of imbalance, for the rest of his life. This condition is every climber's worst nightmare. But Alain put aside his fears. Maybe he couldn't walk a straight line on flat ground, but he was still determined to climb!

WHAT DO YOU THINK?

SINCE SKYSCRAPER CLIMBING IS DANGEROUS, SHOULD IT BE ILLEGAL? SHOULD CLIMBERS BE PUNISHED? WHY OR WHY NOT?

ALAIN ROBERT CLIMBING CHICAGO'S SEARS TOWER, 1999

STUNT 3

CLIMBING THE WORLD'S TALLEST TOWER

On August 20, 1999, Alain climbed Chicago's Sears Tower. At the time it was the tallest building in North America, coming in at 1,454 feet tall! His climb to the top of the 110-story building became the hardest of his life.

Alain arrived at the Sears Tower before dawn. Since it was illegal to climb, he waited until the guards were changing shifts. Then Alain began the climb. Slowly and carefully he scaled the heights. He kept rising, but it was a struggle. He was sweating. His muscles ached. The damp weather made the building's glass panels slick and slippery. His hands and feet kept losing their grip. Suddenly, there was a break in the clouds! Alain glimpsed the summit ahead, and with a last big push, he made it up to the top. Alain raised his two arms and gave a very long, super-loud, victorious roar. Then he fell to his knees, toppled over, and dropped facedown to the concrete roof! But the relief was short-lived. The police were waiting—as usual!

DID YOU KNOW?

The Sears Tower, built in 1974, is now called the Willis Tower. Its steel frame is covered with a curtain wall of dark tinted glass. For more than 20 years it was the world's tallest skyscraper. No longer the tallest, it still has the most space on the inside.

STUNT 4 TAIPEI 101

Taipei 101, in Taiwan, was the tallest building in the world at the end of 2004. Officials invited Alain to climb the skyscraper on Christmas Day, 2004, to help mark the opening. The occasion was a national event, with large crowds and many important government officials present. TV and newspaper photographers hovered around. Although Alain preferred to climb without a safety belt, he reluctantly wore one when the event organizers insisted. The climb proved incredibly hard. The day was rainy and windy, and the weather only got worse as he climbed. An earlier surgery had weakened his left hand. The glass panes that covered the outside of the tower were set an inch or two inside the steel frame. That left only a tiny space to grasp with his fingers and stand on with his toes. Getting past the thick joints was close to impossible! Instead of the two hours Alain expected it to take to reach the top, the climb took about four hours. But he was victorious!

JOKE

CAN A KANGAROO JUMP HIGHER THAN A SKYSCRAPER?

YES. SKYSCRAPERS CAN'T JUMP AT ALL!

ROBERT CLIMBING TAIPEI 101, TAIWAN, 2004

ROBERT UNDER ARREST IN MOSCOW, RUSSIA, 2007

DEFYING DEATH... AND THE LAW!

Alain Robert is only five feet, five inches tall, and weighs 105 pounds. Yet he is super powerful. He can do three pull-ups in a row, holding on with just one finger. Most professional athletes need both hands to do the same thing! But his many climbs haven't come without a cost—he has done irreparable damage to his body over the years. His elbows no longer open, the two long bones in his forearm do not meet properly, his wrists have limited movement, and he cannot straighten his fingers.

Throughout Alain's long career, he did many legal climbs. But many others were against the law. For these, he had to dodge guards and avoid capture. Altogether, the police stopped and arrested him more than a hundred times! He also served some time in jail—including six days in China, seven days in the United States, and nine days in Japan.

JOKE

WHY DID KING KONG CLIMB THE EMPIRE STATE BUILDING?

HE COULDN'T FIT IN THE ELEVATOR!

DID YOU KNOW?

From a distance, Taipei 101 looks like the stem of a bamboo plant. It has thick joints dividing the structure into eight sections, one above another. To the Chinese, the number eight means good fortune and prosperity.

9 ERNEST SHACKLETON

> IT IS IN OUR NATURE TO EXPLORE, TO REACH OUT INTO THE UNKNOWN. THE ONLY TRUE FAILURE WOULD BE NOT TO EXPLORE AT ALL.

BORN:
FEBRUARY 5, 1874,
COUNTY KILDARE,
IRELAND

CLAIM TO FAME:
EXPLORING ANTARCTICA

DIED:
JANUARY 5, 1922,
GRYTVIKEN, SOUTH
GEORGIA, ANTARCTICA

BEFORE THE EXTREME...

Ernest Shackleton was born in Ireland but moved to London, England, with his entire family when he was still very young. The family consisted of Mom, Dad, and 10 kids. Ernest was the second born and the oldest son. His father wanted Ernest to follow in his footsteps and become a doctor. But, at age 16, Ernest signed on as a sailor on a freighter. Ernest did very well at sea. By the time he was 24, he was qualified to be captain of any British ship. For some 10 years, he sailed to ports all over the world. Then he began the first of four expeditions to reach the South Pole and explore Antarctica.

DEFYING DEATH!

Twice, Shackleton defied death trying to reach the South Pole. In 1900, he joined an expedition to the South Pole led by Robert Falcon Scott. Shackleton and Scott trekked toward the pole through extremely bad weather and difficult conditions. They got closer to the pole than anyone else had before. But the trip ended badly for Shackleton. His legs hurt, and his teeth and gums felt sore. The doctor on the expedition diagnosed the condition as a serious case of scurvy, a disease caused by a lack of vitamin C. Without treatment, death might result. Shackleton had no choice—he had to hike the many miles back to the ocean and get on a relief ship back to England. It had long been known that oranges, lemons, and fresh vegetables will prevent scurvy. Yet, despite Scott's best efforts to have these foods available to his men, scurvy had occurred. Back home, Shackleton was treated with large amounts of vitamin C and was cured in about a month.

JOKE

WHAT DO YOU GET IF YOU CROSS AN ANTARCTIC EXPLORER AND A VAMPIRE?

FROSTBITE!

DID YOU KNOW?

Antarctica is the continent that covers and surrounds the South Pole. The South Pole lies near the center of Antarctica. It is the coldest region in the world and is mostly covered by ice and snow. Only a few bare, rocky areas can be seen. Under the ice, Antarctica has mountains and valleys, much like other continents.

⭐ EXPEDITION 2 DEFYING DEATH—AGAIN!

In 1907, Shackleton tried for the second time to reach the South Pole. This time he led his own expedition on the ship *Nimrod*. The team spent months studying the weather and the animal life in the water. They made many important scientific discoveries and became the first to climb an Antarctic volcano, Mount Erebus. The rest of the time, they huddled in their cold camp. Finally, the weather grew warmer and they were able to travel. Instead of dogs to pull their sleds, they had ponies. The ponies, however, got sick and could not be used. The men had to turn to the motor car they had also brought along. But the motor car overheated—despite temperatures below freezing! So the men had to walk. After a while, they grew weak. The powerful winds never stopped blowing. The crew did not have enough food, and their feet and hands were frostbitten. It was time to turn back. They were only 97 miles from the South Pole—even closer than Shackleton had reached before! After walking about 1,260 miles, they boarded the *Nimrod* and headed home.

DID YOU KNOW?

A few years after Shackleton turned back for the second time, two others made it to the pole in other expeditions. The first was Roald Amundsen, a Norwegian, on December 14, 1911. The second was the Englishman Robert Falcon Scott, just five weeks later, on January 17, 1912.

COAST TO COAST

Shackleton made his third voyage to the South Pole on the ship *Endurance*. Two teams had already reached the pole since his first two failed attempts, so Shackleton gave himself a new challenge: he would try to cross Antarctica from coast to coast, passing over the South Pole.

The following time line highlights his long, treacherous, two-year ordeal:

1914

The IMPERIAL TRANSANTARCTIC EXPEDITION.

"We were too recalling in the indescribable freshness of the Antarctic that seems to permeate one's being, and which must be responsible for that longing to go again which assails each returned explorer from Polar regions."

THE MAN OF THE MOMENT—SIR ERNEST SHACKLETON, AGED FORTY

August 1
Shackleton's ship *Endurance* leaves London for Antarctica.

November 5
The 28-man crew arrives at South Georgia, an island off the coast of Antarctica. They take on extra coal, warm clothing, and food.

December 5
The team leaves South Georgia, sailing through waters covered with large pieces of tightly packed ice, called floes.

1915

January 18
Endurance gets stuck after battling 1,000 miles of ice-covered water for over six weeks.

May 1
The sun drops below the horizon; for the next four months, it is dark and extremely cold.

October 27
The frozen ice crushes *Endurance*, which springs a leak. Shackleton orders the men to abandon ship. They move the supplies, food, tents, boats, and dogs (brought along to pull the sleds) onto a large floe.

November 21
The *Endurance* sinks as Shackleton cries out, "She's going, boys!"

December 29
Shackleton and his men set up camp on the floe, hundreds of miles from land, with no ship or radio, and little food.

ENDURANCE STUCK IN ICE

March 30

Shackleton orders the starving crew to begin killing the dogs for food.

April 16

Shackleton and his crew arrive at Elephant Island in three lifeboats after rowing for seven days.

April 24

Shackleton and five men row 800 miles from Elephant Island to the whaling station on South Georgia to get help for the men left on the island.

May 10

The Shackleton group lands on South Georgia. They trek across a range of mountains to find a rescue team.

May 23

They head for Elephant Island, but the ice stops them from getting there.

June 10

A rescue ship tries to save the men but turns back. A month later, still another ship heads there, but it, too, fails to reach the island.

August 30

Finally, a small steamship from Chile picks up the men on Elephant Island and ends their 22-month-long ordeal.

ENDURANCE WITH CREW AND DOGS ON ICE, 1916

ERNEST SHACKLETON AND CREW ON ELEPHANT ISLAND, 1916

CREW WAVING TO BOAT IN THE DISTANCE, 1916

Many honor Shackleton for his courage, bravery, ability to lead, and success at triumphing over hardships. But above all he is widely admired for the valiant way he battled the cold, snow, isolation, and the many hidden dangers in Antarctica.

EXPEDITION 4

THE FOURTH AND FINAL EXPEDITION

In 1921, Shackleton set out on his last Antarctic expedition with a small group of men. This time he wanted to map the continent's 2,000-mile coast and do other scientific research. Shackleton was 47 years old at the time. Not long after he set out, disaster struck. The heroic explorer suffered an apparent heart attack on his ship and died. He was buried on his beloved South Georgia Island.

Shackleton never reached the South Pole, yet he is a superhero. He proved that the South Pole is located on land and not beneath a frozen sea like the North Pole. And his notes on Antarctica helped us better understand our world. The expeditions taxed his endurance and tested the limits of his abilities. But he gave it his best try. For that the world honors and reveres him.

WHAT DO YOU THINK?
HOW WOULD INVENTIONS OF THE LAST 100 YEARS HAVE CHANGED SHACKLETON'S EXPEDITIONS TO THE SOUTH POLE?

SHACKLETON'S GRAVE, SOUTH GEORGIA ISLAND, ANTARCTICA

8 BESSIE COLEMAN

> THE AIR IS THE ONLY PLACE FREE FROM PREJUDICES . . . SO I THOUGHT IT IS MY DUTY TO RISK MY LIFE TO LEARN AVIATION.

BORN:
JANUARY 26, 1892,
ATLANTA, TEXAS

CLAIM TO FAME:
FAMOUS STUNT PILOT

DIED:
APRIL 30, 1926,
JACKSONVILLE,
FLORIDA

BEFORE SHE WAS SKYBOUND...

Bessie Coleman was the 10th of 13 children born on a poor cotton farm in Texas. Her mother was black; her father, a Cherokee Native American. Like other poor farm kids, Bessie had a hard life. Her mother took in washing to help pay the bills. Bessie helped her. She also picked cotton in the fields alongside her parents. School, when she could go, was held in a one-room wooden shack. And it was a four-mile walk from her house. But Bessie was good at math, and she was determined to graduate. After high school, she went to college. But the money ran out after one term and she had to quit. Her dream of more education was shattered. Yet Bessie was not discouraged. She had her heart set on succeeding in life, and succeed she would!

DETERMINED TO FLY!

World War I started in 1914, just one year after Bessie had to drop out of college. She read about how airplanes, a recent invention, were helping to win the war, and began to think of becoming a pilot. But most aviation schools did not accept African American students. They had whites-only rules. Bessie heard that there were better opportunities for black people in the north. Two of her older brothers were living in Chicago. So she joined them, determined to learn to fly!

She applied to almost every flying school in America. And she was turned down by each one for two reasons and two reasons alone: she was black, and she was a woman. French people, however, seemed to be much more accepting. So Bessie applied to France's most famous flying school and was accepted. In November 1920, after learning French, Bessie sailed from New York to France to begin her studies. This was quite an achievement for someone with little money or schooling. In only seven months, on June 15, 1921, Bessie Coleman became the first woman to get an international pilot's license!

BESSIE COLEMAN'S PILOT'S LICENSE, 1921

DID YOU KNOW?

A Frenchwoman, Raymonde de la Roche, had become the world's first female pilot a few years before Bessie. She was nicknamed "The Flying Baroness" in a news article, and was introduced as "Baroness" to everyone she met. In a plane crash she fractured 18 bones, including eight in one hand—yet continued flying.

 ## Science Revealed!

All airplanes are based on the same three principles of flight: a way to hold the plane up in the air, a way to move the plane forward, and a way to steer the plane up and down and from side to side.

The *wings* bulge out on top. As the plane moves, the air rushes faster over the curved tops than across the flat bottoms. That makes the plane rise and stay up as long as it is moving.

The first planes used *propellers* to pull them forward. Today's planes mostly use jet engines, which push, instead of pull.

The *tail*, or rear of the body, steers the plane. The *rudder* turns the plane from side to side and the *elevator* guides the plane up or down.

JOKE

WHY DO PILOTS ALWAYS HAVE WORK?

THEY ARE GOOD AT "LANDING" JOBS!

STUNT 1 ▸ BECOMING "QUEEN BESS"

On September 3, 1922, Bessie Coleman presented her first air show at an airport on Long Island, New York. The weather was warm and sunny. A large crowd gathered. Bessie looked glamorous in her goggles, leather cap, and fur-trimmed flight jacket. The young woman put on a spectacular show. She flew the plane upside down. She twisted, spun, and tumbled around at high speeds. She made huge loop the loops and figure eights in the sky.

Her boldest act was the "Plunge of Death." In mid-flight, Bessie headed the plane straight down, nose first. It looked like the engine had stopped. The crowd seemed sure that she would crash. But, seconds before striking the ground, she pulled back the stick and gunned the engine. The plane pulled out of the dive and headed back up. Everyone cheered Bessie's brush with death!

More air shows followed. As many as 3,000 customers at a time paid to see her fly! The newspapers crowned her "Queen Bess." Bessie Coleman and her incredible flying machine ruled the sky.

Queen Bess also "ruled" her audiences. Black people and white people watched her shows together. At many other public gatherings, the races were separated. The "queen" of flying was also the "queen" of equal rights.

JOKE

WE'D LOVE TO TELL YOU A PILOT JOKE, BUT WE CAN'T.

IT WOULD JUST GO OVER YOUR HEAD!

STUNT 2

BRAVE BESSIE GOES DOWN IN HISTORY

In 1926, Bessie bought a new airplane. Before taking the plane for a test flight, Bessie said a short prayer. Then she got into the rear open cockpit and asked her mechanic to pilot the plane. About 10 minutes into the flight, the engine sputtered and failed. The plane went into a deep nosedive at about 3,000 feet. At 2,000 feet it suddenly flipped over.

Bessie always wore a seat belt. But she was not wearing one this time. She fell out of the plane and died instantly. The plane crashed, killing the mechanic. Later, experts found the cause of the accident: The mechanic had accidentally left a wrench in the engine. It had jammed the controls and felled the plane.

Bessie Coleman died on April 30, 1926, in Jacksonville, Florida. She was only 34 years old. Thousands attended her funeral. Another service was held in Chicago, where she is buried.

DID YOU KNOW?

For many years, on the anniversary of her death, black pilots flew over Bessie Coleman's grave and dropped flowers to honor this great lady. Bessie had not lived long enough to fulfill all her dreams, however. She never opened a flying school for black people, for example, though she had hoped to. That remained for others to do. But she did pave the way for people of color and women to succeed in aviation.

FIVE TRAILBLAZING WOMEN IN AVIATION

In addition to Bessie Coleman, there were many other outstanding women in early aviation history. At the top are these five:

 1 Amelia Earhart, 1867–1930—first woman to fly across the Atlantic Ocean

 2 Ruth Nichols, 1901–1960—set women's world speed, altitude, and distance records

 3 Janet Bragg, 1907–1993—first black woman to earn a US commercial pilot's license

 4 Anne Morrow Lindbergh, 1906–2001—first licensed glider pilot in the US

 5 Willa Brown, 1906–1992—first woman to earn both a pilot's license and a commercial license—outside of France!

7 FELIX BAUMGARTNER

> SOMETIMES YOU HAVE TO BE UP HIGH TO UNDERSTAND HOW SMALL YOU ARE.

BORN:
APRIL 19, 1969,
SALZBURG, AUSTRIA

CLAIM TO FAME:
FIRST MAN TO SKYDIVE
FROM SPACE

PRESENT HOME:
ARBON,
SWITZERLAND

BEFORE ADVENTURES IN THE SKY...

Felix Baumgartner was always a daredevil. While still very young, he pestered relatives to toss him high up in the air—again and again. At age five, Felix drew a picture that showed him dangling from a parachute. Far below, his family waited for him to land. His mother saved the drawing, and years later she gave it to Felix after his first skydiving adventure. By age 16, he was already living the dream he'd had as a very young child. He joined a local skydiving club. He and the sport fit well together. He was strong and able to withstand the stresses of jumping. Although willing to take great risks, he was not reckless. He was always cautious and well prepared. After graduating from high school, Felix enlisted in the Austrian army. He became part of a parachute-exhibition team. The members performed in public air shows. Jumping daily, Felix perfected his skydiving and parachuting skills. He never stopped chasing his dream. As the tattoo on his arm reads, he was "Born To Fly."

Skydiving is the extreme sport of jumping from an airplane, helicopter, high-flying balloon, or another great height. Skydivers use their bodies to control the direction of their fall—before landing by parachute.

STUNT 1

THE ENGLISH CHANNEL

By the time he left the army, Baumgartner was a champion skydiver, but he wanted to take his dream even further. One day, inspiration struck: he would be the first person to skydive across the English Channel! Almost all skydivers head in one direction—straight down. But to skydive the English Channel, and survive to tell the tale, Baumgartner would have to head down and across at the same time!

Baumgartner trained for three years. He had himself strapped to the top of a speeding airplane to get the feeling of flying through the air. He also attached a light, plastic, airplane-like wing to the back of his jumpsuit so he could fly forward while heading down.

On July 31, 2003, Baumgartner left in a small plane from Dover, England. He had the six-foot-wide plastic wing attached to his jumpsuit, an oxygen tank to help his breathing, and a parachute for the landing. When the plane reached a height of almost five and a half miles, he jumped. It was freezing cold and the clouds were so thick that he could not see the land or water below. When he was down to a height of just over one mile, he finally spotted lights on the French coast. He continued to fly at a speed of 220 miles per hour. At about a fifth of a mile above the ground, he opened his parachute and slowly drifted down to land in France. Baumgartner's dive carried him a full 22 miles from the coast of England to France, and lasted 14 minutes.

DID YOU KNOW?

The English Channel is the body of water between England and France. It is about 350 miles long and between 21 and 100 miles wide.

JOKE

YOU DON'T NEED A PARACHUTE TO SKYDIVE ONCE.

YOU ONLY NEED A PARACHUTE TO SKYDIVE TWICE!

THE BIG JUMP

It took Baumgartner five years to get ready for his biggest, scariest, and most dangerous challenge. He wanted to set a new skydiving record—from a height of 24 miles above Earth! To jump from that height, Baumgartner needed a crew of engineers, test pilots, and doctors to help. But first he had to answer two questions:

1 How could he reach a height of 24 miles above Earth?

> Build a giant balloon and fill it with helium gas. Helium is lighter than air and rises in air, like bubbles in water. The balloon would then carry Baumgartner, in a capsule, up to the right height.

2 How could he breathe in the very thin, cold air at that level, called the stratosphere?

> Wear a pressurized space suit like those worn by astronauts. The pressure in the suit could be the same as the pressure at Earth's surface. And the air inside the suit could be heated to a comfortable temperature.

After two practice jumps—one from a height of nearly 14 miles and the other from more than 18 miles—he was finally ready!

Sunday, October 14, 2012, was a historic day for Baumgartner—and everyone interested in space. Baumgartner entered the capsule and the engineers inflated the balloon. The balloon and capsule rose slowly, taking nearly three hours to rise 24 miles.

Finally, the door opened, and Baumgartner looked up at the blackness of space and down at planet Earth. Then he dropped facedown with arms and legs spread open—like a snow angel. Thanks to the suit he did not feel or hear anything. Suddenly, Baumgartner began spinning very fast. If the blood rushed to his feet, he would black out. If it went to his head, it could kill him. So Baumgartner twisted his body to break the spin—and it worked. He dropped faster and faster—100 . . . 300 . . . 600 miles per hour. When he reached 700 miles per hour, he was moving at *supersonic* speed. That is faster than the speed of sound, which is about 650 miles per hour at that height! At a top speed of almost 834 miles per hour, he broke the sound barrier. It produced a noise like thunder, called a sonic boom.

Baumgartner slowed down as he entered the thicker air of Earth's lower atmosphere. The superfast drop lasted less than five minutes. At about a mile above the ground, he opened the parachute and gently floated down. A smoke flare marked the landing zone. Baumgartner made a perfect landing!

JOKE

WHAT IS THE HARDEST PART OF SKYDIVING?

THE GROUND!

Science Revealed!

Twenty-four miles above Earth is within the layer of the atmosphere called the stratosphere, which extends from about 6 to 30 miles above Earth. The air in the stratosphere is much thinner than the air at Earth's surface. At a height of 24 miles, it is almost 1,000 times thinner than on Earth. Airplanes cannot fly nearly this high. Also, the air is very cold.

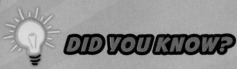
Baumgartner's biggest challenge when jumping from the stratosphere had nothing to do with jumping. In fact, everything about this daring feat was fine—except for the space suit. Baumgartner found it too heavy and hard to move in. It made him feel itchy and antsy. Baumgartner visited a psychologist. He told him that he could not bear long hours inside the space suit. Yet he wanted to jump. Skydiving was very important to him. The psychologist helped Baumgartner get used to wearing the suit. After some time, Baumgartner felt ready to try again. He returned to his team and set out to make the jump. Baumgartner's dislike of being in the space suit came from a condition known as "claustrophobia" (klawss-truh-FOH-bee-uh), which is a strong fear of being in a small, enclosed space.

FELIX BAUMGARTNER IN PRESSURIZED SPACE SUIT, 2012

A DREAM COMES TRUE

Daredevil Baumgartner became world famous. Some eight million people watched the video of his dive. He triumphed over one of the greatest challenges in extreme sports. Scientists collected one hundred million bits of data from his body as he fell at supersonic speeds. The information added much to their understanding of the human body. It showed that humans could safely break the sound barrier outside an aircraft.

But Felix Baumgartner held his skydiving record for only two years. Then, almost exactly two years later, Alan Eustace, an engineer, broke the record. Eustace jumped from a height of 25.7 miles on October 24, 2014—one and a half miles higher than Baumgartner. By then, Baumgartner's skydiving days were over. But he still wanted to face danger and conquer fear. Since he stopped skydiving, he has raced motor cars and tried helicopter racing, among other extreme sports.

6 SIR EDMUND HILLARY

> I AM A LUCKY MAN. I HAVE HAD A DREAM AND IT HAS COME TRUE.

BORN:
JULY 20, 1919, TUAKAU,
NEAR AUCKLAND,
NEW ZEALAND

CLAIM TO FAME:
**FIRST PERSON TO CLIMB
TO THE TOP OF MOUNT EVEREST**

DIED:
JANUARY 11, 2008,
AUCKLAND,
NEW ZEALAND

BEFORE CLIMBING GREAT HEIGHTS . . .

As a child, Edmund Hillary was small and lonely. Ed, as he was called, and his younger brother, Rexford, did household chores and worked on the family farm. They also helped their father with his business of raising bees. Ed was not a very good student, but he read a great deal. He especially loved adventure stories. When he started high school, he was smaller than others his age. But at age 16, Ed had a growth spurt. He shot up to a height of 6 feet, 5 inches. Ed loved climbing, and one year he went on a school skiing trip. From then on, he was hooked on mountaineering. Each year he climbed a different mountain in New Zealand. After two years in college, Ed dropped out. He served in the Royal New Zealand Air Force during World War II. Then he worked in his father's bee business. But his love for climbing kept growing. Soon he was studying mountaineering with experts, preparing to conquer great heights.

CLIMBING THE UNCLIMBABLE

In 1953, Edmund Hillary climbed the "unclimbable" Mount Everest.

Hillary's expedition had a dozen climbers, 35 Sherpa guides, and 350 porters who carried 18 tons of supplies and food. The Sherpas are people who have lived in the high altitudes of the Himalaya mountain range for many generations. They know the mountains well and have guided and carried supplies for many foreigners climbing Mount Everest. The porters carried oxygen for the entire team. Each member of the expedition had several canisters of oxygen gas and a gas mask. Each set weighed about 30 pounds!

The Hillary team began its climb on March 10, 1953. As the men climbed the slope, they set up a series of nine camps at different levels on the mountain for their tents, food, and supplies. Several men stayed at each height while a small team of other climbers continued up. The advance climbers prepared the way for those who followed. They left footprints in the snow, hacked steps into the ice, and left rope ladders. Another advance group then climbed up to the next level, where they set up another camp.

Hillary and his Sherpa, Tenzing Norgay, set up the last, highest camp at 27,900 feet. The two men went to sleep inside the small tent. A howling gale almost blew the tent down the mountainside. The temperature dropped to 30 degrees below zero F! Dawn brought a surprise. Hillary had left his boots outside overnight, and they were frozen solid. He had to warm them for two hours to make them soft enough to wear!

DID YOU KNOW?

Today there is an airport at a level of 9,000 feet up Mount Everest, making the climb shorter and easier. Many thousands of people have successfully reached the summit, and each year many more try.

At 6:30 on the morning of May 29, 1953, Hillary and Tenzing finally set out again. Roped together and carrying ice axes, they slowly whacked their way up the mountain. Suddenly they came upon a huge crevasse—a deep, narrow crack in the ice—as tall as a four-story building. To reach the top of the crevasse, they had to squeeze inside and wriggle up. The men chipped steps in the ice and pulled themselves up. They came to a big hump in the ice, struggled over it, and looked around. There was nothing above them. It was exactly 11:30 a.m. They were at the summit—the first humans ever to reach the top of Mount Everest!

Science Revealed!

Air pressure is the weight of air pressing down on our bodies. The higher up we go on a mountain, the less air there is above us. The pressure is lower. Lower air pressure means less oxygen to breathe. The air at the top of Mount Everest has only one-third as much oxygen as air at sea level. Mountain climbers must carry a supply of oxygen—or they will get sick or die.

SIR EDMUND HILLARY (LEFT), DEREK WRIGHT, AND MURRAY ELLIS AT THE SOUTH POLE, 1956

 EXPEDITION 2

CROSSING THE BOTTOM OF THE WORLD

In 1956, the British geologist Vivian Fuchs invited Hillary to join him on an expedition. It was to cross the 2,158-mile continent of Antarctica from sea to sea. Hillary signed on. He would map Antarctica, study its geology, plan a route across the continent, and set up depots of food, fuel, and supplies for Fuchs's trip over the ice. The journey was dangerous and there were many near accidents along the way. The team traveled on three farm tractors that had been specially outfitted for this trip. Several times the tractors tumbled into deep crevasses and had to be hauled out. By December 1957, Hillary was about 500 miles from the South Pole. He decided to make a quick, unplanned dash for the pole itself. They had barely enough fuel to get there. But, despite many hazards and dangers, they made it! On January 4, 1958, Hillary became the first person to drive to the South Pole.

FROM THE OCEAN TO THE SKY

EXPEDITION 3

After climbing Mount Everest and crossing Antarctica, Edmund Hillary had a new ambition. In 1977, at 58 years of age, he wanted to find the source of the 1,500-mile-long Ganges, the sacred river of India. He called the expedition "From the Ocean to the Sky."

Hillary gathered a team of explorers together and bought three powerful motorboats to carry them up the river. The group set sail from the mouth of the Ganges River in the Bay of Bengal, a part of the Indian Ocean. As they went on, they had to battle the river's wild, white-water rapids. Large rocks threatened to smash the boats. About a thousand miles upriver, they came to a giant waterfall. This left the men no choice: they had to continue on foot. Hillary and the others hiked up to an altitude of about 18,000 feet when Hillary was struck with altitude sickness. Team members radioed for a helicopter that took him to a hospital, where he made a complete recovery.

Hillary's team trekked on for the remaining 7,000 feet. They found the source of the Ganges in a giant glacier high in the Himalayas. Hillary had not completed the whole journey, but experts credit him with the exciting discovery.

 Science Revealed!

Hillary had two important scientific instruments to help guide him across the ice-covered continent of Antarctica—the compass and the sextant. For direction, Hillary used the compass except, of course, when standing at the South Pole. At that point a compass was of little help since every direction he faced was north! The sextant, on the other hand, measured the angle between the horizon and the sun, moon, or a star, which helped him plot his position.

HILLARY (LEFT) AND NEIL ARMSTRONG, 1985

THE LEGEND LIVES ON

Sir Edmund Hillary ranks high among the world's greatest mountain climbers, explorers, and daredevil adventurers. He was the first to climb to the peak of Mount Everest, to cross the entire continent of Antarctica, and to discover the source of the Ganges River. In 1985, Edmund Hillary and astronaut Neil Armstrong flew in a small plane to the North Pole. That made Hillary one of the very few people in the world who stepped on both the North *and* South Poles!

JOKE

DID YOU READ THE BOOK ABOUT MOUNT EVEREST?

IT'S A REAL CLIFFHANGER!

5 HARRY HOUDINI

> I'M JUST A CLEVER GUY GETTING OUT OF STUFF. WHAT THE EYES SEE AND THE EARS HEAR, THE MIND BELIEVES.

BORN:
MARCH 24, 1874,
BUDAPEST, HUNGARY

CLAIM TO FAME:
WORLD'S BEST ESCAPE ARTIST

DIED:
OCTOBER 31, 1926,
DETROIT, MICHIGAN

BEFORE THE CUFFS...

Harry Houdini was born in Budapest, Hungary. His parents named him Ehrich. When Ehrich was four years old, his family came to the United States. As a boy, Ehrich was very athletic, especially as an acrobat and gymnast. He could twist and turn his body into any position. He could also make his muscles grow and shrink in size. At an early age, he could bend over backward and pick up a pin with his teeth! At the age of nine, young Ehrich joined a small circus. His favorite stunts were done on a trapeze that hung from a tree. This was his start in show business. As he got older, Ehrich added magic to his acrobatic acts. He did card tricks, made balls appear and disappear, and pulled coins out of the air. By age 17, he was doing magic acts before paying audiences. That's when he changed his name to Houdini, taken from a famous French magician, Robert-Houdin. Around the same time, he developed an interest in the locks and handcuffs they sold at the gun shop around the corner from his house. This was the beginning of a lifelong interest in escaping from restraints. Houdini would go on to astound audiences throughout the world with the most daring escapes.

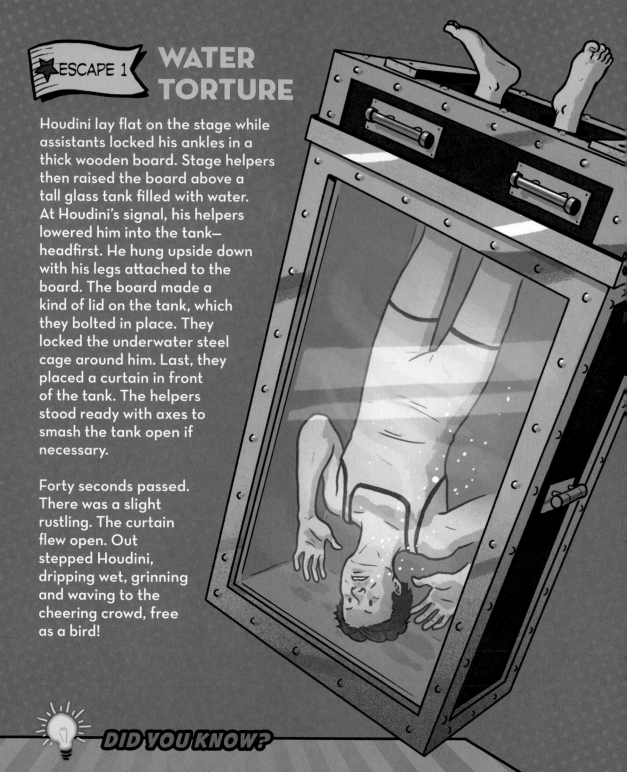

WATER TORTURE

Houdini lay flat on the stage while assistants locked his ankles in a thick wooden board. Stage helpers then raised the board above a tall glass tank filled with water. At Houdini's signal, his helpers lowered him into the tank—headfirst. He hung upside down with his legs attached to the board. The board made a kind of lid on the tank, which they bolted in place. They locked the underwater steel cage around him. Last, they placed a curtain in front of the tank. The helpers stood ready with axes to smash the tank open if necessary.

Forty seconds passed. There was a slight rustling. The curtain flew open. Out stepped Houdini, dripping wet, grinning and waving to the cheering crowd, free as a bird!

DID YOU KNOW?

Most people can hold their breath for about one minute underwater. Houdini was able to go without breathing more than twice as long.

MILK CAN

ESCAPE 2

Before Houdini performed this particular stunt, he addressed the audience. He told them he had trained himself to hold his breath for very long periods of time. Then Houdini put on a bathing suit. He climbed into a three-foot-tall milk can filled to the brim with water. A giant stopwatch on stage stood ready to count down the minutes. Houdini lowered himself into the can with his head underwater. Helpers used six locks to bolt the lid in place. An assistant signaled the audience to hold its breath. He started the clock and placed a curtain in front of the can.

After about 30 seconds, most people in the audience were gasping for breath. But Houdini's head remained under the water. A helper kicked the can to let Houdini know that a minute had passed. At a minute and a half, the audience grew restless. They were afraid that Houdini was in trouble. After three minutes, people demanded an end to the trick! They feared that Houdini would die. Armed with an ax, a helper moved forward to break open the tank. But Houdini did not need to be rescued. Instead, he pulled back the curtain. Stepping forward, he shook off the water. He had broken free of the locks—and held his breath underwater for more than three minutes!

HARRY HOUDINI INSIDE A GIANT MILK CAN, ST. LOUIS, MISSOURI, 1908

97

THREAD THE NEEDLES

To start the stunt that Houdini called Needle Trick, he asked audience members to look into his open mouth. Sure enough, it looked empty. Next, he held up 50 sharp, pointed needles and 60 feet of thread. As the people watched, he swallowed the needles and thread! Then he washed everything down with a glass of water. Incredible! For a few seconds, Houdini moved his jaw from side to side. He slowly opened his mouth. With a trace of a smile, he pulled out the thread. It was hard to believe. The needles were all lined up and hanging from the thread!

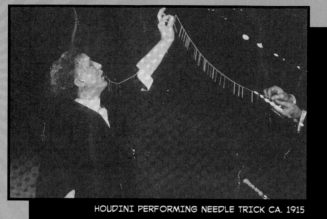

HOUDINI PERFORMING NEEDLE TRICK CA. 1915

 Secret Revealed!

Houdini, like most magicians, never told the secrets of his trade. But three years after his death, an assistant explained the famous Needle Trick. Before every performance, Houdini placed the threaded needles between his teeth and cheek. When audience members checked his mouth, he held it open with his fingers. His fingers hid the needles and thread, making them impossible to see. Then Houdini just *pretended* to swallow the separate needles and thread with a glass of water! But what he really did was spit them into the glass. The reflection of the water and his hand holding the glass hid them from view. To everyone's great wonder, Houdini then reached into his mouth and pulled out the thread—with the needles attached that he hid before the performance! Remember: knowing the secret does not mean you can do the trick. This trick is very dangerous. It took Houdini many years to master. Whatever you do, *don't try it at home*!!!

JOKE

WHAT DO YOU CALL AN OWL THAT CAN GET OUT OF HANDCUFFS?

HOOODINI!

INSIDE THE BELLY OF A WHALE

In 1911, a dead whale washed up on a beach in Boston. Some businessmen challenged Houdini to escape from inside the whale's body. Not one to refuse a dare, Houdini had some police officers lock him in handcuffs and leg irons. They then placed him, helpless, inside the whale's body. Assistants then sewed up the belly of the whale. They also wrapped the whale's body in heavy chains.

For a thrilling 15 minutes, no one saw or heard from Houdini. When the time was up, he burst out of the whale and took a bow. His hands were free of handcuffs and there were no irons on his legs. Little did the audience know that Houdini nearly suffocated and died from fumes inside the whale!

WHAT DO YOU THINK?

THE YEARS AROUND 1900 WERE A PERIOD OF GREAT IMMIGRATION. HOUDINI'S FAMILY CAME TO THE UNITED STATES, ALONG WITH MILLIONS MORE FROM ALL OVER THE WORLD. THE NEW ARRIVALS WERE FLEEING CROWDED CITIES, HARSH LAWS, AND TERRIBLE LIVING CONDITIONS. ESCAPE AND FREEDOM WERE ON EVERYONE'S MIND.

HOUDINI'S ESCAPES MAY HAVE REMINDED PEOPLE OF THEIR SEARCH FOR FREEDOM AND THEIR OWN DANGEROUS JOURNEYS FROM THE OLD COUNTRY TO THE NEW WORLD. DO YOU AGREE OR DISAGREE WITH THIS IDEA? WHY?

HOUDINI INSIDE CRATE, BEING LOWERED INTO
THE EAST RIVER IN NEW YORK, JULY 1914

ESCAPE 4

DEFYING DEATH!

In this trick, helpers locked Houdini in handcuffs and leg irons. They placed him in a large wooden box loaded with 200 pounds of lead. Then they nailed shut the box cover, wrapped the box in chains, and lowered it into New York's East River. No one could see that Houdini had prepared one side of the box with two loose boards that formed a trapdoor.

While the helpers were lowering the box, Houdini had time to wiggle free of the handcuffs and leg irons. Once on the river bottom, he planned to squeeze out through the trapdoor and swim to the surface.

One time, though, the trick nearly did not work. The box sank very deep into the muddy river bottom. Houdini could not open the trapdoor! As he struggled to free himself, he felt himself running out of breath. Finally, with only seconds to spare, he broke free! He shot up to the surface— and gulped a deep breath of fresh air!

FINAL BLOW

Houdini had a powerful build. He bragged that he could take punches to his belly and feel no pain. A backstage visitor once asked him if this was true. Houdini said it was. But before he could tighten his muscles, the visitor struck four hard blows to Houdini's belly. At his performance that evening, Houdini complained of stomach pain. The next day medics took him to the hospital. Doctors said the punches had released strong poisons in his body. A few days later Houdini was dead. Though he died nearly 100 years ago, he is still very well known. His name continues to pop up near the top of most every list of greatest daredevils of all time, and probably will do so for the next 100 years!

4 PHILIPPE PETIT

> I STARTED, AS A YOUNG, SELF-TAUGHT WIRE WALKER, TO DREAM OF NOT SO MUCH CONQUERING THE UNIVERSE, BUT, AS A POET, CONQUERING BEAUTIFUL STAGES.

BORN:
AUGUST 13, 1949,
NEMOURS, FRANCE

CLAIM TO FAME:
TIGHTROPE WALKER
BETWEEN TOWERS

PRESENT HOME:
WOODSTOCK,
NEW YORK

BEFORE WALKING THE TOWERS...

At age four, Philippe Petit enjoyed climbing trees, fences, furniture, or anything at all. When he was six years old, he taught himself to do magic tricks. And on his 17th birthday, he turned to juggling and tightrope walking. After a year of walking on tightropes, Philippe added stunts to his walks—from turning somersaults, to riding bicycles and unicycles, to jumping through hoops. School was not Philippe's greatest interest. At 18, he dropped out and left home. He earned money on the streets doing magic tricks and juggling. One time, a bad toothache brought Philippe to a dentist's office. In the waiting room he came across a newspaper article about two tall towers being built in New York City. Philippe vowed to walk a tightrope between those two towers one day, and he did!

NOTRE DAME CATHEDRAL

The Cathedral of Notre Dame is to Paris, France, what the Twin Towers of the World Trade Center were to New York City in the United States. When Petit was 22 years old, he was living in Paris. He felt the cathedral's two towers calling to him. They told him to stretch a wire between them and walk across. Petit spent lots of time at the cathedral getting ready. He took secret measurements and noted the guards' schedules. He sneaked into parts of the cathedral that were not open to the public. And he studied the tops of the towers to decide how to attach a wire from one to the other.

Late one night in June 1971, most of Paris was fast asleep. Petit made his way into Notre Dame with a few friends. Some climbed up to the roof of one tower, some to the roof of the other. From his tower, Petit tied a fishing line to a rubber ball and threw it to the other tower. His friends on the other tower attached the steel cable to the fishing line and Petit pulled it back to his tower. They all spent the rest of the night fastening the ends of the cable on both roofs, from tower to tower.

Early the next morning, Petit made his way onto the wire—250 feet above the ground. A crowd gathered below. They looked up silently. Could he do it? Or would he slip and fall? But Petit walked carefully, step after step. He juggled three Indian clubs. He danced a little. The worried silence was replaced by loud cheers and applause. Petit stepped off the wire at the second tower. Instead of friends, he was met by police and arrested. It was his first arrest, though there were many more to come. Newspapers all over the world covered Petit's daring adventure. They called him a brave, brilliant daredevil.

PHILIPPE PETIT LYING DOWN ON THE TIGHTROPE BETWEEN THE TOWERS OF NOTRE DAME, PARIS, FRANCE, 1971

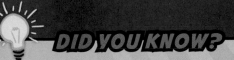

DID YOU KNOW?

The Cathedral of Notre Dame stands on a small island in Paris's Seine River—a fine example of twelfth-century architecture. The building is decorated with hundreds of stone carvings placed very high above the ground. It is said that only an angel can admire their details.

By January 1973, Petit was ready to realize the dream he had to cross a tight wire between the Twin Towers of New York City's World Trade Center. Walking between the towers was against the law. So Petit made all of his preparations in secret.

Petit visited the buildings about 200 times over three months. Since the towers were still under construction, he sneaked in wearing different disguises. Sometimes, dressed as a construction worker, he figured out how to bring in all the equipment he needed. Other times, dressed as a businessman, he checked out the guards and workers. One time, Petit posed as a writer for a French architecture magazine. He went up to the roof of one tower to see where he would attach the wire!

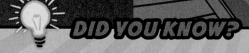
DID YOU KNOW?

On September 11, 2001, hijackers in airplanes destroyed New York City's World Trade Center. The World Trade Center, which opened on April 4, 1973, consisted of seven buildings, including the so-called Twin Towers. When finished, the Twin Towers were the tallest buildings in the world—taller than the Empire State Building. Their highest point was a third of a mile high.

The night before the walk, Petit and the others set up shop on the top of the North Tower. They used a large bow and arrow to shoot a long cord across to the South Tower. The men on top of the South Tower used the cord to pull across a heavier cord, and then a thick, heavy rope. With this strong rope they stretched the 450-pound steel-cable wire from one tower to the other a quarter mile above the street.

Just before seven o'clock on the morning of August 7, Petit began walking across the wire. He wore his usual black outfit and soft shoes. And he carried a long, heavy balance pole. Petit stepped onto the wire with great confidence. Within moments, he was dancing on the wire. He kneeled and waved to the people watching from all over. Then he stopped, lay down on his back on the wire, and got up again. Over the next 45 minutes, he made eight crossings on the wire. At the end, many arms reached out to help him, though he protested proudly that he needed no help! The police got a "Man on Wire" call and arrested Petit. But since he was a popular figure who agreed to do some free tightrope walks for children, they dropped all charges.

His crossing between the Twin Towers became one of the best-known daredevil stunts of all time. Newspapers, books, and television shows told of the most extraordinary event! In September 2015, a movie about Petit, called *The Walk*, was released.

DEFYING THE LAW

On June 3, 1973, Petit made five back-and-forth walks across a wire strung between two towers of the Sydney Harbour Bridge in Australia. The police arrested and fined him $200. But he decided to have some fun with the police. While learning to juggle he had become an expert pickpocket. So, during the arrest, he stole an officer's watch—which he immediately returned! It is supposed that Petit has been arrested some 500 times for his daring—and illegal—tower tightrope walks!

JOKE

HALFWAY BETWEEN TOWERS, THE SCARED TIGHTROPE WALKER SAID, "I CAN'T TAKE ANOTHER STEP FORWARD."

"THEN JUST WALK BACK!" SOMEONE SHOUTED.

PETIT TIGHTROPE WALKING TOWARD THE EIFFEL TOWER, PARIS, FRANCE, 1989

After Petit's three *illegal* high-wire walks, he was invited to do *legal* walks all around the world. They included walks at the Louisiana Superdome (United States), the Cathedral Church of Saint John the Divine (United States), the Paris Opera (France) and the inclined walk to the Citadel of Vauban (Namur, Belgium). Other performances were Walking the Harp/A Bridge for Peace (Israel), Tokyo Walk (Japan), Viennalewalk (Austria), Farinet Funambule! (Switzerland), and Historischer Hochseillauf (Germany).

In August 1989, the mayor of Paris invited Petit to help celebrate the 200th anniversary of the French Revolution. Petit decided to make the walk even more dangerous and exciting than usual. He would walk on a cable that stretched up at a sharp angle, from the ground to a point high on the Eiffel Tower.

He anchored the wire at the base of the historic Chaillot Palace. It rose, crossed over the Seine River, and ended on the second level of the Eiffel Tower, 38 stories above the ground. Petit walked the nearly half-mile length of the wire. Tens of thousands of people watched from the streets below. Later, the mayor of Paris greeted and honored him. All of France celebrated his courage.

3 EVEL KNIEVEL

> ANYONE CAN JUMP A MOTORCYCLE. THE TROUBLE BEGINS WHEN YOU TRY TO LAND IT.

BORN:
OCTOBER 18, 1938,
BUTTE, MONTANA

CLAIM TO FAME:
WORLD-FAMOUS
MOTORCYCLE STUNT RIDER

DIED:
NOVEMBER 30, 2007,
CLEARWATER, FLORIDA

BEFORE HE JUMPED...

Evel Knievel was born Robert Craig Knievel in the copper-mining town of Butte, Montana. At age eight, he saw the Joie Chitwood auto daredevil show, which toured the United States thrilling audiences with daredevil stunts. Although very smart, Knievel often landed in trouble. When he was a teenager he got arrested. The jailers nicknamed Knievel "Evil Knievel." But Robert changed the spelling to Evel because he thought it looked better. The next time he got into trouble, the police gave him a choice: join the army or go to jail. He chose the army. After he got out, remembering the auto daredevil show from his youth, Evel put on his own motorcycle daredevil show. For several years, Knievel performed around the country. A good number of his acts ended in injuries. But he became a celebrity and got lots of publicity. People couldn't get enough of Evel Knievel, and he never lacked for enthusiastic audiences, earning him the moniker "King of the Daredevils."

TOP FIVE DEATH-DEFYING ACTS!

Over and over, Knievel's motorcycle jumps tempted death. Some acts succeeded; some missed. Here are five of his most famous close calls.

1 On February 10, 1966, in Barstow, California, Knievel introduced a new trick. He stood absolutely still while another motorcycle rider speeded straight at him. At the very last possible instant, Knievel jumped up high. But it was too late. The motorcycle struck and threw him 15 feet in the air. He spent nearly a month in the hospital.

2 For a 1966 performance in Missoula, Montana, Knievel jumped over 12 cars and a van. But he had too little speed and he crashed. The accident broke Knievel's left arm and several ribs.

3 On October 13, 1968, in Carson City, Nevada, Evel aimed to leap over only 10 cars, but he missed and crashed after clearing the ninth. He slid and banged into his parked truck. A broken right shoulder and left hip were the results.

4 On May 10, 1970, in Yakima, Washington, Evel planned to jump over 13 Pepsi-Cola delivery trucks. In the approach, he rode over a patch of grass and could not get up to speed. He landed on his front wheel and was thrown from his bike. He broke both legs, his right arm, and his collarbone.

5 On May 26, 1975, before 90,000 people—his largest audience—Knievel tried to set a new world record by jumping over 13 buses. He easily cleared the first 12 buses, but the motorcycle came down sideways at the 13th bus and he crashed. Tossed over the handlebars, Knievel broke his back, pelvis, and right hand, and suffered a concussion!

EVEL KNIEVEL CRASHING HIS MOTORCYCLE TRYING TO JUMP 13 BUSES, LONDON, UNITED KINGDOM, 1975

KNIEVEL JUMPING OVER FOUNTAIN AT CAESARS PALACE, LAS VEGAS, NEVADA, 1967

 **JUMP 1**

THE CRASH HEARD 'ROUND THE WORLD

On a visit to Las Vegas in 1967, Knievel saw the fabulous fountains at the Caesars Palace casino. He wanted more than anything to jump over those fountains, so he called Jay Sarno, owner of Caesars Palace. After many attempts to convince Sarno, he finally set December 31, 1967, as the date for the event.

Knievel started the show with his usual warm-ups and practice rides. Finally, he was ready for the jump. Knievel zoomed toward the takeoff ramp at full speed. He zipped straight up the ramp at 90 miles an hour—and easily flew through the fountains' spray. But then, just inches away from a safe landing, Knievel slammed onto the edge of the landing ramp! The motorcycle handlebars were ripped out of his hands. He fell off the bike and tumbled end over end at top speed, hurtling forward and skidding on the pavement. He came to a sudden, hard stop against a brick wall in the parking lot. Knievel crushed his pelvis and thigh bone in the accident. He broke his hip, a wrist, and both ankles. And he had a concussion that left him in a coma for nearly a month!

Somehow, Knievel recovered. A film he had made of the jump was shown on TV's *Wide World of Sports*. The crash became the most famous motorcycle event in history. Knievel's name and reputation spread widely. Crowds flooded every appearance. He earned as much as $25,000 for each performance!

SNAKE RIVER CANYON

On a plane trip in 1971, Knievel saw the huge Snake River Canyon, near Twin Falls, Idaho. He knew at once he had to jump there. But there was a problem. Even Knievel's most powerful motorcycle could not carry him across the three-quarter-mile-wide canyon. So Knievel ordered a rocket-powered motorcycle. It looked more like a rocket than a motorcycle and was named Skycycle X-2. A built-in parachute would open for a smooth landing after crossing the canyon. In test runs, the Skycycle could not make it all the way across the canyon. Knievel gave it less than a 50-50 chance of success! But he was still determined to try.

On September 8, 1974, millions of people around America packed movie theaters to see the jump as it happened. Newspapers delayed publication to include the result. At exactly 3:36 in the afternoon, Knievel got into Skycycle and pushed the starter button. The engine roared to life, and the rocket took off. At the same instant, the parachute burst out and opened! Still, the Skycycle made it only partway across before falling slowly into the canyon. One of Evel Knievel's most daring acts of courage had failed. Luckily, he escaped with just minor injuries.

 DID YOU KNOW?

Despite all of his accidents and failed jumps, Knievel managed to set a new world record on February 28, 1971, in Ontario, California. He jumped over a lineup of 19 automobiles! This event appears in the movie *Evel Knievel.*

NEW WORLD RECORD

On October 25, 1975, just five months after his unsuccessful jump over 13 buses on May 26, 1975, Knievel was back atop a motorcycle. But this time, he had some good luck. He attempted to jump 14 buses at the Kings Island theme park in Ohio. Although the frame of his Harley-Davidson motorcycle actually broke, Knievel managed to land safely past the 14th bus! Having jumped a distance of 133 feet, Knievel set a new record for making the longest successful jump on a motorcycle. The record held for 24 years. The number of people who watched the Kings Island jump was the highest in the history of *Wide World of Sports*.

JOKE

DID YOU HEAR THE ONE ABOUT THE ANGRY BUS DRIVER?

HE JUMPED HIS BUS OVER 13 MOTORCYCLES!

KNIEVEL SUCCESSFULLY COMPLETING A JUMP OVER 14 BUSES, KINGS MILLS, OHIO, 1975

THE FINAL JUMP

In January 1977, Knievel signed up for a truly amazing jump—it was over a tank filled with sharks. The act would be shown live on coast-to-coast TV. During a rehearsal, Knievel lost control of his motorcycle and crashed into a TV cameraman. He broke both of his arms, but the cameraman lost one of his eyes! The crash marked the end of Knievel's career as a motorcycle daredevil. He spent the rest of his life, until his death at age 69, making public appearances and selling Evel Knievel souvenirs. The *Guinness Book of World Records* says he suffered more broken bones than any other person—435—throughout his life!

2 DAVID BLAINE

I'M GOING TO PUSH MYSELF AS FAR AS I CAN.

BORN:
APRIL 4, 1973,
BROOKLYN, NEW YORK

CLAIM TO FAME:
ENDURANCE CHAMPION OF THE WORLD

PRESENT HOME:
NEW YORK CITY

BEFORE HE CHEATED DEATH...

David Blaine decided to become a magician at age five when his mother gave him a deck of cards. Later he read a book about doing card tricks. But by the time he was a teenager, David Blaine was already a skillful magician. At first he mostly performed magic tricks at parties. Then he worked as a magician in nightclubs. In 1997, he was seen in a TV special, *David Blaine: Street Magic*. In it, he did astonishing magic tricks on a New York City street before baffled onlookers. Then Blaine began to move beyond doing magic tricks. Instead, he started performing stunts of endurance that would put his life in chilling danger . . .

STUNT 1 · BURIED ALIVE

On April 5, 1999, Blaine stepped into a plastic box shaped like a coffin, to be buried alive. Workers closed the box and placed it inside a six-foot-deep hole under a New York City street. On top of the box, they put a three-ton, clear plastic tank filled with water. That's 6,000 pounds of extra weight! Blaine remained inside the box, under the water tank, for an entire week. He breathed oxygen that was pumped into the box and had a buzzer to use in case of an emergency. He ate nothing and sipped only two or three tablespoons of water a day. In the course of a week, about 75,000 people stopped to peer down at him. On the seventh day, reporters from around the world gathered. A crane lifted up the water tank. Workers took the lid off the box, and hundreds of cheering spectators surged forward. They were burning with curiosity. How would he look after his long burial? Would he be able to move and speak? Well, fortunately they didn't have to wait very long for their answer. Soon Blaine sat up, smiled, and greeted the cheering crowd. *Phew!*

DID YOU KNOW?

Harry Houdini, an earlier daredevil, had attempted the "Buried Alive" stunt in his lifetime, but was not successful. He died in 1926 without performing this feat in public. To this day, Blaine is the sole master of this most amazing test of endurance.

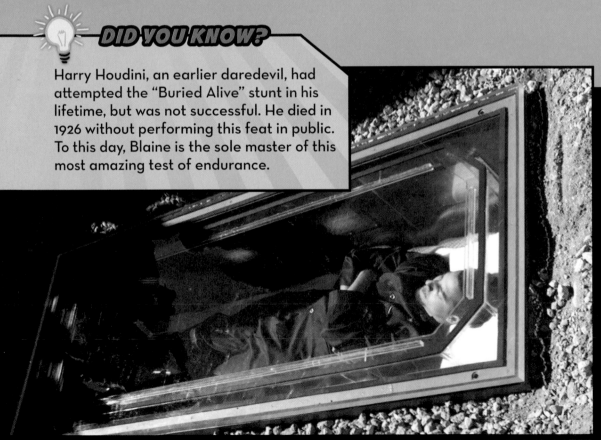

DAVID BLAINE BURIED ALIVE, NEW YORK CITY, NEW YORK, 1999

DID YOU KNOW?

Blaine was always working to strengthen his endurance. On April 30, 2008, he held his breath for a Guinness World Record of 17 minutes and 4 seconds. Compare that to Houdini, who could only hold his breath for a little longer than 3 minutes. The latest record is now up to more than 24 minutes!

 STUNT 2

FROZEN IN TIME

It was early in the morning on November 27, 2000. Blaine was inside an eight-foot-tall block of ice to see how long he could survive. The ice had been chopped from a glacier and shipped from Alaska to Times Square in New York City. Workers had hollowed out the center. Inside the ice, Blaine was shirtless, with only boots, cargo pants, and a wool stocking cap to keep him warm. In addition to openings at the top and bottom, there was a small hole for tubes to bring him air and liquids. Day and night, Blaine stood upright in this icy prison. More than 1,000 people an hour lined up to catch a glimpse of the man on ice. For two and a half days, the public filed past, waving and shouting. Usually, Blaine smiled back.

It rained the evening of the third day. He had been locked in ice for 63 hours, 40 minutes, and 15 seconds. Weak and pale, he decided to end the stunt. Workers freed him with a chain saw. They wrapped him in a robe and blanket and placed him on a stretcher. And they took him by ambulance to a doctor's office. It was a month before Blaine could walk again. But his Frozen in Time stunt made headlines around the world and set a world record for endurance!

BLAINE INSIDE HIS BLOCK OF ICE, NEW YORK CITY, NEW YORK, 2000

DID YOU KNOW?

...laine's record stood for nearly ten ...ears. Finally, in 2010, it was broken ... Israeli magician Hezi Dean.

WHAT DO YOU THINK?
SOME SAY BLAINE IS A SUPER MAGICIAN WHO JUST MAKES PEOPLE BELIEVE THAT HE CAN DO THE IMPOSSIBLE. OTHERS SAY THAT HE ACTUALLY DOES THE IMPOSSIBLE. WHAT DO YOU THINK—AND WHY?

 ★ STUNT 3

ABOVE THE BELOW

Blaine stepped into a tall, narrow, clear plastic box. The date was September 5, 2003. He hoped to set a record for the longest time a person could go without food. Workers lifted the box with a crane, raised it high in the air, and kept it there for the length of the feat. Blaine sat in his perch for exactly six weeks and two days. He ate nothing and only sipped a little water through a tube every day. Blaine's stunt was even broadcast on television. People watched him survive starvation day after day. Some spoke out against the stunt. They said he was making fun of starving people around the world.

Forty-four days into the stunt, the crane lowered Blaine to the ground as 10,000 people watched. It tipped the box forward and he stepped out. Surprisingly, he needed only a little help. Blaine had lost nearly one-third of his weight! And it took six months to recover his good health.

 ## Science Revealed!

Scientists who have studied how long a person can live without food tell us that it varies from person to person. In general, a person can live without food anywhere from 45 to 61 days. But most cannot survive beyond 10 to 14 days without water or something else to drink.

ELECTRIFIED

Electrified was Blaine's gutsiest stunt of all. The stunt began on October 5, 2012. For three days, Blaine stood on a small platform atop a 22-foot pillar erected on Pier 54 in the Hudson River in New York City. He surrounded himself with seven large, electrical Tesla coils. When turned on, the coils zapped him with one million volts of electricity! Onlookers were baffled. How could Blaine be struck by electricity that looked like lightning—and remain standing?

Blaine wore a steel, chain-mail bodysuit. His feet had chain-mail socks; his boots, metal soles. An open wire cage covered his head. When the Tesla coils were on, lightning-like sparks shot between the coils and Blaine's hands and feet. It was awesome! But Blaine was not hurt because the lightning bolts sent electricity through the metal suit around his body instead of through it. Blaine was safe as long as he stood still. But what if he reached inside his helmet to scratch his nose? The electricity would flow through him and deliver a jolt that might electrocute or even kill him.

The hardest part of this stunt was standing still in a 27-pound suit for three days. At the end of the time, assistants helped him into an ambulance. Blaine wondered if he'd ever be able to top this stunt!

BLAINE PERFORMING ELECTRIFIED, NEW YORK CITY, NEW YORK, 2012

DID YOU KNOW?

In 1891, Nikola Tesla found a way to transmit electricity without wires. He invented a coil that produced high-voltage bursts of electricity. As the electricity arced through the air, giant lightning bolts shot out from the coil. Blaine used several Tesla coils in his stunt. The artificial lightning zapped Blaine—but did not hurt him.

JOKE

THE "ELECTRIFIED" STUNT DID NOT KILL BLAINE.

BUT THE ELECTRICITY BILL NEARLY DID!

WHAT'S NEXT?

Blaine has millions of fans around the world. People know his name and his stunts from TV and one-person shows. He shocks and amazes audiences with his ability to endure the worst conditions and has set several world records for endurance. Yet he continues to work hard every day to come up with new ways to thrill audiences and boggle their minds. So what's next for this daredevil? We'll have to wait and see!

1 AMELIA EARHART

ADVENTURE IS WORTHWHILE IN ITSELF.

BORN:
JULY 24, 1897, ATCHISON, KANSAS

CLAIM TO FAME:
MOST FAMOUS FEMALE PILOT OF ALL TIME

DIED:
JULY 2, 1937, DISAPPEARED IN THE PACIFIC OCEAN

BEFORE SHE FLEW...

Amelia was born in Atchison, Kansas, where she spent her early childhood. Amelia and her sister, Muriel, liked doing things that most girls were not allowed to do at that time. The sisters played ball, climbed trees, explored new neighborhoods, and fished in nearby streams. Amelia's father wanted his daughters to be brave—even though he was later afraid to fly! One time, Amelia and Muriel saw a roller coaster at a fair and decided to build one themselves. Amelia took the first ride. The crate slid down so fast that it flew off the track! She shouted, "It's just like flying!" Little did she know, she would soon be doing just that! Amelia was only six years old in 1903, when the Wright brothers built the first powered airplane. When she saw an airplane for the first time at age 11 she called it "a thing of rusty wire and wood." But when the airplane took off, she was thrilled beyond belief. Her first chance to be a passenger in an airplane came when she was 23. She knew the moment it left the ground that someday she would be a pilot and fly her own plane!

FLIGHT 1 ⭐ SETTING A RECORD

Amelia Earhart took her first ride in an airplane in 1920 and was immediately smitten. Determined to be a pilot herself, she worked odd jobs so she could pay for flying lessons. After only one year of lessons, Amelia bought herself a secondhand plane that was painted bright yellow. She named it *Canary*. At age 24, she took the necessary tests and was awarded her pilot's license in December 1921. She wasted no time and, in October 1922, flew the *Canary* to set a record as the world's highest-flying female pilot! She reached an altitude record of 14,000 feet—a brave and daring accomplishment. The next year she scored another triumph, when she earned an international pilot license.

 ## FLIGHT 2 ⭐ DANGER AHEAD

In April 1928, Amelia Earhart was offered the chance to fly across the Atlantic Ocean as a passenger in an airplane. It was a once-in-a-lifetime opportunity and Earhart wanted desperately to go. She knew the flight would be dangerous and wrote a will—just in case. Sure enough, the flight ran into difficulties. The door lock broke, the oil tank leaked, the weather was stormy, and both engine and radio did not work properly. Still, the plane finally landed safely in England, making Earhart the first female passenger to fly across the Atlantic Ocean.

When Amelia was asked about her flight as a passenger on the transatlantic flight, she said, "I was just baggage, like a sack of potatoes." But once back in the United States, she was hailed as a great hero. New Yorkers honored her with a parade and she was invited to the White House to meet President Calvin Coolidge. Newspapers nicknamed her "Lady Lindy," which was based on "Lucky Lindy," a name given to Charles Lindbergh, who was the first pilot to fly across the Atlantic the year before.

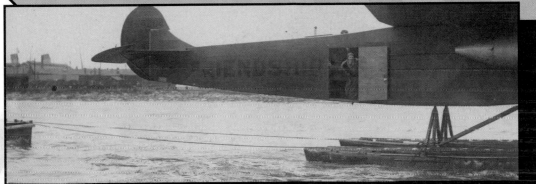

AMELIA EARHART LEANING OUT THE CABIN DOOR OF THE PLANE, *FRIENDSHIP*, SOUTHAMPTON, CALIFORNIA, 1928

 FLIGHT 3

WITH FLYING COLORS

After this 1928 flight, Amelia planned a second Atlantic flight, far bolder and riskier than the first. For this second flight, she would pilot a plane, alone, from North America to Europe.

Amelia took off on this historic flight on the morning of May 20, 1932, from Newfoundland, Canada, in the hope of landing in Paris, France. But she ran into trouble almost immediately. The altimeter, an instrument that measures altitude, stopped working. Flames sputtered out from the single engine, and ice formed on the wings as she flew higher to avoid stormy weather. The weight of the ice made the plane spin and plummet down some 3,000 feet. Working furiously, Amelia pulled out of the dive and continued the flight. She flew nearly 15 hours without stop, help, or rest. Then the engine started to fail. It seemed clear that she would not make it to Paris. So, Amelia made an emergency landing in a farmer's field in Northern Ireland. She had not reached her goal, but she had crossed the Atlantic Ocean. She became the first woman to fly the Atlantic in the longest, fastest, nonstop, solo flight to that date!

Science Revealed!

Advances in science made Amelia's flight across the Atlantic Ocean possible. Most important were the improvements that made newer planes more powerful and more reliable than the old ones. The new planes could carry enough fuel to fly longer distances. Two-way radios allowed pilots to report their progress and communicate with people on the ground. The invention of special compasses for airplanes, as well as more accurate charts, or maps, helped pilots more in their missions. And finally, better methods of weather forecasting gave early warnings of storms and suggested routes to avoid them.

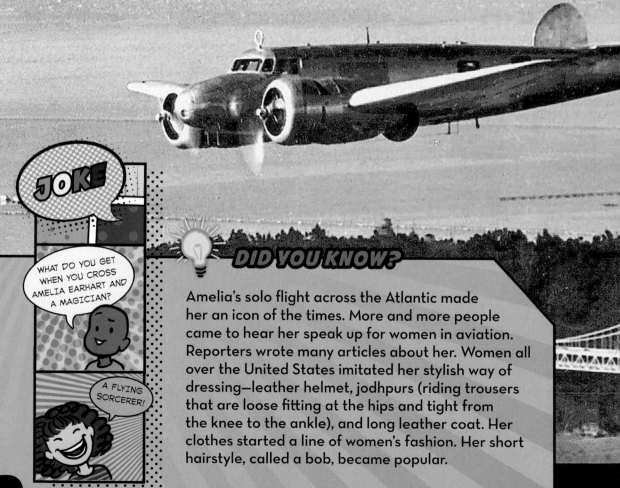

JOKE

WHAT DO YOU GET WHEN YOU CROSS AMELIA EARHART AND A MAGICIAN?

A FLYING SORCERER!

DID YOU KNOW?

Amelia's solo flight across the Atlantic made her an icon of the times. More and more people came to hear her speak up for women in aviation. Reporters wrote many articles about her. Women all over the United States imitated her stylish way of dressing—leather helmet, jodhpurs (riding trousers that are loose fitting at the hips and tight from the knee to the ankle), and long leather coat. Her clothes started a line of women's fashion. Her short hairstyle, called a bob, became popular.

THE DISAPPEARANCE

Amelia still had one more major goal in mind: to fly all around the world, roughly following the equator. She told everyone that it would be her last long flight. Amelia would be the only pilot, but she wanted someone else on board to help navigate. She chose Fred Noonan, an expert pilot and aerial navigator, to chart the course and help operate the radio. Earhart took off from Oakland, California, on March 17, 1937, in a two-engine propeller plane. She headed west to Hawaii for the first leg of her round-the-world flight and landed there safely. After three days in Hawaii, she left on the next leg. However, during the takeoff, the plane lurched, resulting in too much damage for it to continue. She had to postpone the rest of the flight.

On June 1, 1937, Amelia tried her round-the-world flight once more. This time she left from Miami, Florida, and flew east, following the equator in the opposite direction from her original route. She headed southeast to Brazil. Then she crossed the Atlantic Ocean to Africa and passed over Asia on the way to Australia. By June 29, Earhart had reached New Guinea, an island just a little north of Australia. Millions around the world followed every detail of the flight. They read daily reports of her travels. They even knew of the hot cocoa and oranges she had while flying! By the time Amelia got to New Guinea, she had flown 22,000 miles. That left only 7,000 more miles to go. Her next stop was tiny Howland Island—2,500 miles away, only two miles long, and one mile wide. But it would be the most difficult part of the trip—crossing the Pacific Ocean. To be safe, she took on extra fuel.

Amelia Earhart left New Guinea on July 2 and was never heard from again.

EARHART'S PLANE DURING A TEST FLIGHT, OAKLAND, CALIFORNIA, 1937

UNSOLVED MYSTERY

No one knows what happened to Amelia Earhart. Did the plane run out of fuel and crash into the ocean? Or did something else occur? For a long while, planes and ships searched for her but they found nothing. Her disappearance remained an unsolved mystery. On January 5, 1939, she was declared legally dead. The US government declared that Amelia's plane had plunged into the ocean as she tried to reach Howland Island—and failed.

But for the next 80 years, people pondered the mysterious disappearance of Amelia Earhart. The mystery suddenly became front-page news when, on July 2, 2017, a photo was found that people thought might show Amelia Earhart on Jaluit, a tiny island in the middle of the Pacific Ocean. The grainy photo shows a seated woman with her back to the camera. She looks a little like Amelia. It also shows a standing man with a hairline like that of Fred Noonan. One expert in analyzing hard-to-understand photos says it is "very likely" that the photo shows Amelia and Fred. Also, in the background is a plane on top of a barge, similar to the plane Amelia had been flying. Still, others deny that this photo was even taken during the year of her disappearance.

PL-MARSHALL ISLANDS, JALUIT ATOLL, JALUIT ISLAND. ONI #14381
JALUIT HARBOR.

The mystery continues. Some say she landed on an island but not Jaluit. Others say that the photograph was from a different time and does not show Amelia at all. Still others are looking elsewhere for evidence of where the plane might have crashed.

There is one point, though, on which everyone agrees: Amelia Earhart was a true daredevil, one of the greatest who ever lived. She was a courageous and passionate pilot. She is among the most important people in aviation history who set many world records. And she did all this while women were struggling for greater acceptance.

During her lifetime, Amelia Earhart was beloved by millions around the world. She was—and still is—an inspiration to young men and women to take chances and strive to fulfill their wildest ambitions.

WHAT DO YOU THINK?
WHY DO PEOPLE KEEP PUZZLING OVER THE LAST FLIGHT OF AMELIA EARHART?

INDEX